The Philosophy Book for Beginners

The
Philosophy
Book *for*
Beginners

A Brief Introduction to Great Thinkers and Big Ideas

SHARON KAYE, PhD

ILLUSTRATION BY BEA CRESPO

ROCKRIDGE
PRESS

For general information on our other products and services or to obtain technical support, please contact our Customer Care Department within the United States at (866) 744-2665, or outside the United States at (510) 253-0500.

Rockridge Press publishes its books in a variety of electronic and print formats. Some content that appears in print may not be available in electronic books, and vice versa.

TRADEMARKS: Rockridge Press and the Rockridge Press logo are trademarks or registered trademarks of Callisto Media Inc. and/or its affiliates, in the United States and other countries, and may not be used without written permission. All other trademarks are the property of their respective owners. Rockridge Press is not associated with any product or vendor mentioned in this book.

Interior and Cover Designer: Brian Lewis
Art Producer: Janice Ackerman
Editor: Annie Choi
Production Manager: Michael Kay
Production Editor: Melissa Edeburn

Illustration: ©2021 Bea Crespo

Author photo courtesy of Sally Al-Qaraghuli

Paperback ISBN: 978-1-64876-532-2
eBook ISBN: 978-1-64876-533-9

R1

For Tris, Audrey, and Xavier,
with all my love.

Contents

Part Three: Axiology   89

Chapter Eight: What Makes a Good Life?   91

Chapter Nine: How Do I Decide What's Right? 103

Chapter Ten: What Do I Owe to the World?   115

Chapter Eleven: What Makes a Society Just? 125

Introduction

Dear Reader,

Thank you for opening this book. It offers an important message: your whole life up to this moment has been a dream. All your memories are false. Nothing around you really exists. Furthermore, your own body is part of the illusion. You have no idea who or where you really are. Nevertheless, the time has come for you to complete your mission—just kidding!

. . . Or maybe not. The scenario I just described is possible. Although it may seem far-fetched at first, on closer examination, the scenario raises some deeply important questions. What is truly real? How do I know? Has my life been determined in advance? Who am I? What am I supposed to be doing?

If you have ever seriously considered questions like these, you are not alone. You are a philosopher.

What Is Philosophy?

The word *philosophy* comes from the Greek words for "love of wisdom." Philosophers have existed since human beings began wondering about the world around them and making theories to explain their experiences. However, philosophy became a movement during the golden age of ancient Greece through the thinking of an extraordinary man: Socrates.

Socrates lived in Athens in the fifth century BCE. He was proud of his city-state for establishing the world's first democracy. But he was disturbed by how fragile this new kind of government could be. If the people were going to rule themselves, they needed wisdom.

Socrates questioned the teachers, lawyers, politicians, priests, and other authorities of Athens and found they were not as wise as they claimed to be. In fact, they were more interested in *appearing* wise than in actually *being* wise. (Sound familiar?) Socrates was forced to conclude that he was the wisest man in Athens simply because he was willing to admit that he was not wise!

The youth of Athens hailed Socrates like a rock star for pointing out the failings of society's authorities. In retaliation, these authorities arrested Socrates for corrupting the youth and not believing in the right gods. At the trial, the jury found Socrates guilty. Though his friends offered to help him escape, Socrates insisted on accepting his death sentence.

Fortunately, this attempt to snuff out philosophy backfired. Outraged by his execution, Socrates's followers established a school called the Academy at which both men and women could raise questions, propose theories, and debate issues. The Academy was the world's first university. It was official—human beings were on a quest for wisdom.

Why Philosophy?

More than two millennia have passed since the start of the Academy. Our society has come a long way (consider the fact that we officially abolished slavery), but we still have a long way to go (slavery continues to exist unofficially). Philosophy can help in at least three ways.

Philosophy provides a common ground. Society has gone global. We live and work with people from vastly different cultures. We cannot expect to agree with one another about God or the meaning of life, but we can all strive for wisdom. Like Socrates, the wise person begins by admitting how little they really know. This knowledge is a solid basis for appreciating a diversity of perspectives and uniting in the search for truth.

Philosophy helps us express our deepest beliefs. Socrates was not the only persecuted philosopher. Sadly, many of the authors discussed in this book were censored, punished, tortured, or killed for speaking their minds. Society will always try to silence us. But we must never be silenced. A philosopher who really strikes a chord with you will help you develop and voice your own philosophy.

Philosophy promotes listening. At his trial, Socrates famously said, "The unexamined life is not worth living." Once you realize how hard it is to examine your life, you should become more interested in how other people do it. By debating the big questions, you can become an honorable adversary. In martial arts, we thank our opponents for challenging us to improve. The same is true in philosophy.

With the staggering advancement of technology, the power to save or destroy humanity is at our fingertips. Managing this power requires democratic cooperation. Socrates's mission was to fortify democracy by loving wisdom. This mission is more important now than ever.

How to Use This Book

Philosophy is traditionally divided into four branches:

Metaphysics: the study of reality (what is real?)

Epistemology: the study of knowledge (what can we know?)

Axiology: the study of value, which include ethics (how should we live?) and aesthetics (what is beauty?)

Logic: the study of reasoning (how can we make good arguments?)

Most philosophical issues involve more than one of, if not all, the branches. For example, the question of whether free will is real or an illusion is a metaphysical question. But it might prompt you to ask how to identify an illusion in the first place, which is an epistemological question. Furthermore, someone might argue that free will is real because morality requires it, which brings us to ethics. Finally, all philosophical discussion should be reasonable—as determined by the rules of logic.

This book highlights the greatest ideas from around the world in the first three branches of philosophy. Logic is better studied separately, since it is a skill rather than a body of ideas. However, we will have occasion to mention some especially important logical principles. Likewise, bear in mind that philosophy is not the same as religion. Although both subjects may concern God, faith, and the meaning of life, religion presupposes belief whereas philosophy questions belief.

Each chapter will end with a thought experiment, which is a hypothetical situation designed to explore the implications of a theory. Whereas scientists test physical substances in the lab, philosophers use their imaginations to test ideas. Thought experiments do not need to be realistic to do their job. At the age of 16, Albert Einstein imagined what a beam of light would look like if you were chasing it at the speed of light. This thought experiment led to his discovery of relativity. You can use the thought experiment at the end of each chapter to challenge old assumptions and make space for new ways of thinking.

Two philosophies popular today are stoicism and existentialism. Stoics believe that wisdom means living in accordance with cosmic harmony, indifferent to pleasure and pain. Existentialists believe that wisdom means living authentically by taking responsibility for free choices. These two contrasting approaches have their roots in a variety of perspectives from across the globe. Understanding these ideas, and understanding philosophy in general, requires the examination of influential philosophers throughout history.

The men and women featured in the following pages are the cream of the crop—geniuses who built on one another's work and inspired humanity to improve. But learning about their contributions will be pointless unless *you* enter the story. What insights can you glean from them?

Sapere aude! This famous philosophical motto means "Dare to be wise!" May this book be a platform for you to develop your own philosophy of life. Standing on the shoulders of giants, you will see farther than you thought possible.

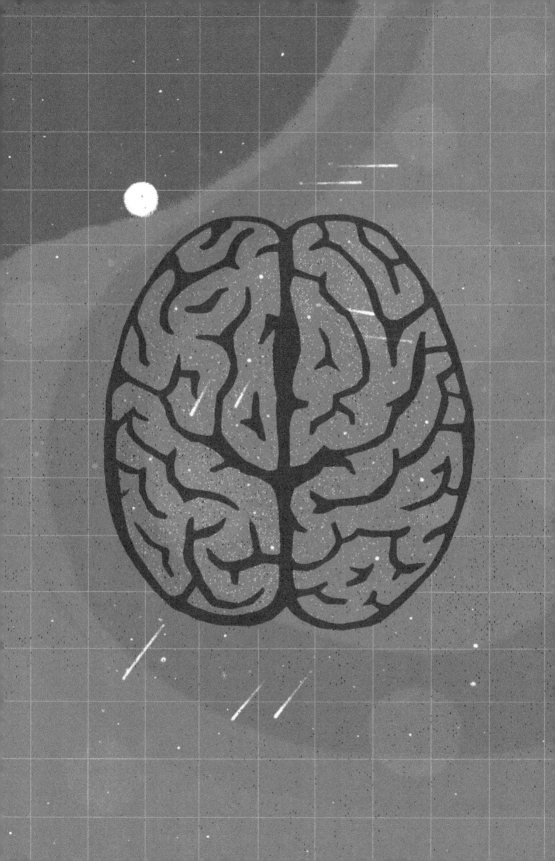

PART ONE

Metaphysics

Metaphysics is the branch of philosophy concerned with theories of reality. Good philosophers do not make up outrageous ideas for shock value. They explore the options for belief and try to find reasonable answers to the most important questions about life.

When I was a kid, my best friend and I loved to lie on the grass and look up at fluffy white clouds floating through blue sky. One day, it occurred to me that she might see the clouds as red. We both learned to call the clouds "white," but that didn't mean we saw them as the same color. All our colors might be reversed. From that day on, I became very interested in whether other people see things the same way I do.

What questions about life do *you* deem most important? As you read about the philosophers in the following chapters, take note of the questions that concerned them and ask yourself whether you find their answers plausible.

CHAPTER ONE

What Is Truly Real?

In physics we learn that the universe is made up of atoms. We have pictures of these amazing little things. They are real. End of story . . . for the physicist.

For the philosopher, atoms are just the beginning of the story. Their existence raises a host of further questions: Where did they come from? Why are they the way they are? How do they turn into complex beings like you and me? Are complex beings only determined by their atoms, or is something else going on? What, if anything, lies beyond atoms? Even granting that atoms *seem* real, are they truly real?

Pressing questions about human life may lead us to wonder about the physical world.

Adi Shankara–Karma

Have you ever asked yourself: Why was I born into *this* life instead of another? Why do I have *this* body and these parents? Why do I live *here* instead of in a better place? Why can't I be smarter, stronger, richer, or more beautiful like other people? Was it just chance that determined the circumstances of my life?

According to Hindu belief, your life circumstances are not due to chance but to *karma*. Karma is the law of nature that rewards good behavior and punishes bad behavior. For example, if you give to charity this week, you may meet a new friend next week. If you hurt someone today, you may get sick tomorrow.

Since we receive most of our life circumstances at birth, Hindus infer that we must have lived a past life. The law of karma ensures that we receive the next life we deserve. This explains the inequality we observe among humans and gives us incentive to live a good life–so that the circumstances of our next life will be better.

The theory that human beings have an everlasting soul which passes through a succession of physical lives is called *reincarnation*. Reincarnation raises the question, what exactly must we do to improve our life circumstances?

The eighth-century Hindu philosopher Adi Shankara believed that focusing on the physical world causes us to cycle downward in the karmic wheel. When we are attracted to material things, we behave badly in order to acquire them. This behavior causes us to suffer in this life and into the next.

In order to cycle upward, Shankara said we must reject the physical world and believe only in Brahman. Brahman is not a god. Worshipping gods may help us resist the allure of material goods, but all gods are ultimately a projection of the physical world. To escape the physical world altogether, we must conceive Brahman as an eternal absolute. Shankara argued that, if Brahman is completely nonphysical, it must be completely formless and therefore beyond human comprehension.

We do not need to comprehend Brahman to believe in it and ultimately experience it. Whereas action always leads to further entanglement is the physical world, the practice of meditation over time can lead to Brahman. Enlightenment, also known as "nirvana," occurs when we achieve consciousness of the nonphysical and formless nature of reality. In nirvana we experience that only Brahman is truly real and that we are one with Brahman.

Adi Shankara has been a tremendously influential voice in Eastern philosophy—conceptions of wisdom originating in Asia. However, he shows some remarkable parallels to Plato, one of the most influential voices in Western philosophy, which originated in Europe.

Plato—Idealism

Look around you for an example of perfection. Find one? Not likely. Even the loveliest flower has blemishes if you look close enough. Perhaps it is not surprising that the world is so flawed—what is really surprising is that the human mind, despite being surrounded by imperfection, is able to conceive of perfection at all.

How is it that I can see "in my mind's eye" a perfect triangle, even though every single triangle I have ever encountered in the world is imperfect? How is it that I can conceive of perfect equality, even though I have never seen two perfectly equal things?

Plato found this situation deeply suspicious. For him, in the fourth century BCE, it was a sure sign that the physical world is just a shadowy reflection of the ultimate reality.

Plato was Socrates's most devoted follower and primary founder of the Academy. According to legend, he posted a sign over the entrance of the Academy that said, "Let no one who is ignorant of mathematics enter here." Plato loved math because of its perfection; math captures the ideal forms of things. For example, you can design a bridge using mathematical formulas. If you build it, the result will reflect the formulas, even if it doesn't match exactly.

Math also reveals the mind's grasp of ideals. Picture yourself trying to learn the Pythagorean theorem ($a^2 + b^2 = c^2$). At first it seems confusing, but you think about it, draw some sketches, plug in some numbers, examine a proof, and realize that it *has to be true*. "Aha!" you exclaim.

Plato regarded this "aha!" moment as an important clue. When we discover the truth, it feels familiar, like running into an old friend on the street. "Aha!" we say. "John—I almost didn't recognize you." Just as our bodily eye recognizes an old friend, our mind's eye recognizes the truth. This ability suggests that our minds are nonphysical entities, or souls, that have access to a reality beyond the physical world.

Drawing on the theory of reincarnation, Plato sometimes suggested that each human soul must have lived a past life—not in the physical world, but in a nonphysical world of perfect forms. Other times, Plato suggested that the "world of forms" is not actually a world, but a state of mind human beings can achieve through contemplation.

One way or the other, Plato was convinced that only the perfect forms of things are truly real. This is metaphysical idealism. The imperfect examples around us exist only as shadowy reflections of these eternal, unchanging ideals.

Aristotle—Realism

Plato's star student at the Academy was Aristotle, who fittingly disagreed with Plato over just about everything.

Uninterested in perfection and the world of perfect forms, Aristotle just wanted to understand how things work. For example, how do things grow? Consider a puppy. At birth, he fits in the palm of your hand. Six months later, he's too heavy to lift. How did a little food and water each day make this happen? Why didn't the food and water turn the puppy into a tree? Why is the puppy able to move around but a tree cannot?

Today, we know these answers thanks to the science of biology. But Aristotle was one of the first people to ask these questions, which is why he is known as the father of biology. Answering biological questions requires getting your hands dirty—which Aristotle did. He had a laboratory, he collected samples, he dissected specimens, he made observations, and he classified types. He was a scientist at heart.

Yet Aristotle was not satisfied identifying how individual things worked. He wanted to understand the common principles underlying everything in order to construct a unified picture of how the universe as a whole works. In the end, he proposed that every existing thing is explained by four causes:

The **material cause** is the stuff an object is made of. An eyeball is made of flesh.

The **formal cause** is the ideal shape of an object. Here Aristotle adapts Plato's notion of "perfect forms." If an eyeball is damaged, it's not going to work anymore. The "ideal eyeball" is a structure for maximal eyeball functioning.

The **efficient cause** is the moving force behind an object. You are the efficient cause of your eyeball. An eyeball floating in a jar will not work, even if it is undamaged. It must be attached in the right way to an agent in order to function.

The **final cause** is the reason for an object. The purpose of an eyeball is to see. It can also be used as food or as a paper weight, but these secondary functions will not explain what an eyeball *is*.

Aristotle's *doctrine of the four causes* works best on the parts of animals, which was his original application. But he tried to use it to explain everything—with interesting results. (Hint: try using it to explain *yourself*!) If we call Plato a "metaphysical idealist," we can call Aristotle a "metaphysical realist." For him, the physical world is truly real.

Margaret Cavendish—Materialism

Although Aristotle clearly pronounced the physical world to be real, he did not clearly indicate whether the physical world was the *only* reality. What about the soul that both Plato and Adi Shankara believed in? What about God, heaven, or any kind of eternal realm beyond what we see around us? Could reality be both physical and nonphysical? Aristotle allowed for this possibility.

But the 17th-century English philosopher Margaret Cavendish did not. She boldly argued for materialism (also known as physicalism): the view that only the physical world is truly real.

This view is striking for two reasons. First, it was extremely difficult for a woman to become a philosopher prior to the 20th century. Because women were routinely denied access to education and libraries, Cavendish represents a rare female voice in the history of philosophy.

Second, Cavendish was working in an aggressively Christian era. Christianity is crucially committed to nonphysical entities and realms, thus making it very tricky for Cavendish to argue against them without getting into trouble.

Her main argument for materialism is ingenious. It can be summarized as follows:

1. All reality is in motion.

2. Immaterial objects cannot move.

3. Therefore, immaterial objects are not real.

Cavendish's conclusion logically follows from her premises—meaning that, if her premises are true, then materialism must be true. But are her premises true?

The first premise, that all reality is in motion, is hard to dispute considering that our planet is hurtling through a solar system, which is in turn hurtling through a galaxy. Under these conditions, has anything ever been still?

The second premise, that immaterial objects cannot move, can be supported with a thought experiment. Imagine an angel flying from one church spire to another. At first, she seems just as conceivable as a bird. On closer inspection, however, we note that her foot goes through the roof and her wings push no air. Since the angel is not physical, she has no grip on her surroundings to propel herself. Cavendish therefore argued:

1. Motion requires interaction by contact.

2. Immaterial objects cannot interact by contact.

3. Therefore, immaterial objects cannot move.

Cavendish was careful to assure the authorities that she had proper faith in all the unreal things religion required.

Meanwhile, setting religion aside, there was only matter for her. Matter moves itself in many different ways. Some matter is capable of the most subtle motion of all—namely, thought.

How is it possible for a brain to think? Thinking seems like a mysterious power. But for Cavendish, thinking is no more mysterious than other powers of matter, such as magnetism. Certain kinds of stone can attract iron. Likewise, certain kinds of flesh can perceive and reflect. It is amazing, but in her view completely natural.

George Berkeley– Subjective Idealism

Whereas Cavendish saw no mystery in matter, 18th-century Irish philosopher George Berkeley found matter intolerably mysterious. In his view, the concept of physical stuff is so fraught with contradictions that we must reject its existence.

What is matter? Materialists speak as though we are surrounded by it. But Berkeley pointed out that we never actually encounter matter—what we encounter are the *qualities* of matter.

Consider an eight ball from the game of pool. It is small, smooth, light, round, black, odorless, tasteless, and makes a loud "crack!" when you hit it against the other balls. The materialist wants to say that the eight ball is a chunk of matter "containing" all the aforementioned qualities. But when we examine the qualities more closely, we see that they cannot be contained in matter.

Think about the color, smell, taste, and sound of the eight ball. These qualities are subjective, meaning that they are in the mind of the perceiver rather than in the object itself.

Berkeley proves this by pointing out that the color, smell, taste, and sound of the ball can vary from person to person.

Bring the ball to an alien who lives on a distant planet. To him, the ball could look pink, smell delicious, taste sweet, and make no sound when hitting other balls. This alien's sensory organs are very different from ours! But who is right and who is wrong? There is no objectively correct answer. Color, smell, taste, and sound are in the perceiver, not in the object.

But what about the first four qualities: small, smooth, light, and round. Surely, an object's size, texture, weight, and shape are the same for anyone who perceives it?

Not so, argued Berkeley. To a microscopic creature, the ball seems huge, rough, heavy, and just as flat as the surface of the Earth seems to us. To a subatomic creature, the ball isn't even a solid object but a swarming cloud of particles, which he can pass right through! Humans have a completely different perception of the ball. Who is right and who is wrong? There is no objective answer. Size, texture, weight, shape, and even solidity are in the perceiver, not in the object.

What is left of the eight ball? All its qualities are subjective. There is nothing left "out there" independent of our minds. The eight ball is not a chunk of matter. It is a perception.

Berkeley applied this analysis to the entire physical world and concluded that it does not exist. Only minds exist. His famous slogan was "To be is to be perceived."

The only remaining question for Berkeley is: where do all our perceptions come from? Being a deeply religious person (and a bishop in the Church of Ireland), he did not need to look far for his answer: God. Only an omnipotent and omniscient creator could project qualities so perfectly coordinated into so many minds. In fact, what an efficient way to create the world! Why create physical stuff to be perceived when you can create perceptions directly?

THOUGHT EXPERIMENT
THE FALLING TREE

From the 18th-century Irish philosopher George Berkeley. If a tree falls in the forest, and no one is around to hear it, does it make a sound? If Cavendish is correct to say that matter exists, then yes. The falling tree makes vibrations, though we may not call these vibrations "sound" when there are no ears to receive them. If Berkeley is correct to say that only perceptions exist, then no. Even the vibrations would require a perceiver in order to be real. (On second thought—does God count as a perceiver? If so, then he would hear the tree.)

CHAPTER TWO

Can the Existence of God Be Proven or Disproven?

Thanks to the courage of free thinkers throughout history like Socrates, who refused to believe in the gods he was supposed to, we now live in an age of religious freedom. Some people believe in a god or gods, others don't—there is no need to justify your choice.

Nevertheless, it is easy to forget that belief or nonbelief *is a choice*. Suppose you grew up in a Catholic family in Detroit. To you, believing in God feels as natural as speaking English. But suppose you were born into a Buddhist family in Nepal instead. Then *not* believing in God would feel just as natural as *not* speaking English.

Although we are able to choose our beliefs, we often just go along with how we happened to be raised. Have you considered the options? As a philosopher, you'll want to examine arguments for and against the existence of God so you can make a choice of your own.

Averroes—The Teleological Argument

Perhaps the most popular reason for believing in God comes from observing purposeful order in the natural world.

Take a deep breath. Isn't it magnificent that the air you breathe is exactly suited for your benefit? Suppose the air had too little oxygen. Or suppose that, in addition to oxygen, it contained a toxic gas. Then human life would become difficult or impossible.

Instead, the contrary is true. We find the air we breathe and the water we drink—the whole environment on Earth— wonderfully harmonious. The sun gives us the seasons, which give us plants and animals, which give us the food and shelter we need.

Can such a brilliant system have come about by chance? The 12th-century Arabic philosopher Averroes argued no.

Picture yourself traveling through the mountains. You catch sight of a rock shaped like a chair. Either it came about by chance or someone made it. Look closely. The qualities you observe in the rock may entitle you to believe it exists for a purpose. Is the rock symmetrical, right-sized, comfortable, aptly placed, etc.? The more evidence you see that the rock is *good for sitting*, the more evidence you have that it was deliberately *made for sitting*.

Likewise, if the qualities we observe in the world are well designed, then we feel entitled to conclude that the world must have had a designer. This is known as the teleological argument because the word *telos* means "purpose."

Averroes himself acknowledged, however, that the teleological argument is not decisive from a scientific perspective. It took many more years of scientific progress to show exactly why.

In the 19th century, the English naturalist Charles Darwin presented his theory of evolution by natural selection. It shows how survival of the fittest creates the *appearance* of design. Darwin's theory is based on four principles:

Replication: Organisms produce copies of themselves.

Random mutation: The copies contain small changes—some that are advantageous for survival.

Harsh conditions: The environment kills off the copies without enough advantages.

Eons of time: With each generation, the small changes add up to big changes.

Imagine the earliest air-breathing creatures. Those who needed more oxygen, or who had a toxic reaction to the nitrogen in our air, struggled to survive. Unable to compete with other creatures that thrived with the existing atmosphere and environment, the struggling creatures failed to reproduce and died out.

The creatures whose needs matched the environment thrived and multiplied. With their unfit competitors dead, they became the success stories we see all around us today. The creatures that survived are magnificently fitted to the natural world—but only by trial and error. You *have to be* magnificently fitted in order to survive.

Is it possible that God created the natural world through this process of trial and error? Sure. But Darwin argued that the process can run itself without the need for any supernatural intervention, leaving us without reason to infer from it that God exists.

Thomas Aquinas— The Cosmological Argument

Even if we agree that the natural world can run itself on the principles of evolution, wasn't someone needed to start the process? Perhaps planet Earth produced life because of its position in the solar system, which in turn took shape due to a cosmic explosion. Still, something had to set off the explosion. What could have done that, other than God?

This line of reasoning is known as the cosmological argument. The 13th-century Italian philosopher Thomas Aquinas is a famous source for this argument.

Note, however, that the argument is sometimes misstated something like this:

1. Everything that exists had to be caused to exist by something else.

2. The cosmos is everything physical.

3. Therefore, the cosmos must have been caused to exist by something nonphysical—God.

Someone who believes in God cannot assert the first premise of this argument. To a believer, God was not caused to exist by something else! God is conceived as an eternal being, meaning that he has existed forever, with no beginning and no end. If you try to argue for God by saying that everything has to have a beginning, you contradict yourself.

Aquinas understood this contradiction. Being a Dominican monk, he followed Christian tradition in accepting by faith that the cosmos had a beginning. But he was careful to point out that it may not have (and he was accused of heresy for this). The cosmos could have existed forever, with no beginning. Though it is difficult to conceive the cosmos as eternal, it is no more difficult than conceiving God as eternal.

Aquinas argued that, even if the cosmos were eternal, God would still be needed to explain how it got moving. He reasoned as follows:

1. Being a mover is active while being moved is passive.

2. Active and passive are opposite states.

3. It is impossible for something to be in opposites states at the same time.

4. Therefore, it is impossible to be a mover and moved at the same time.

For Aquinas, this argument means it is impossible for anything to move itself. Anything in motion must be put in motion by another mover.

But wait—there's more. That other mover, if it is moving, must in turn be put in motion by another mover, and so on, and so on. This process cannot go on to infinity because then the sequence never would have gotten started. Therefore, it is necessary to arrive at a first mover who is *unmoved*.

What could move the cosmos without itself moving? Only a nonphysical being as powerful as God: "The Unmoved Mover."

Notice that Aquinas's argument hinges on the thesis nothing can move itself. But we have seen Margaret Cavendish argue that matter has the power to move itself in many ways. What do *you* think?

Mary Astell—
The Ontological Argument

Both the teleological and the cosmological arguments for God are *empirical*. As we will see in chapter 5, this means they depend on facts about the physical world. Some philosophers, known as *rationalists*, regard the physical world as a poor source of knowledge. They look for arguments that depend on reason and logical principles instead.

The rationalist approach to proving God's existence is called *ontological* from the Greek word for "being." It means that an examination of the nature of God will prove he exists—just like an examination of the nature of a triangle proves the Pythagorean theorem.

The most famous version of the ontological argument comes to us from the 12th-century philosopher Anselm of Canterbury. Anselm began by defining God as "that being than which no greater can be conceived." He went on to argue that God cannot just exist in the mind. If he did, then we could conceive of a greater god—namely, one that exists in the mind *and* in reality. The reader is left with the suspicion that Anselm's awkward definition begged the question, meaning that it *assumed* the very thing it was supposed to *prove*.

English philosopher Mary Astell offered a more straightforward ontological argument in the late 17th and early 18th centuries. She defined God as "that being who is by nature infinite in all perfections." She defined a "perfection" as any quality that is better to have than not have. Her examples of perfections include wisdom, goodness, justice, intelligence, and power.

A definition of *god* often found in dictionaries is "supreme being." Astell would say that what it means to be supreme is to have every perfection without limit. She insisted that even someone who did not believe in God would have to agree that this definition is correct. Hence, she presented the following argument:

1. God has every perfection without limit.

2. Existence is a perfection.

3. Therefore, God has existence without limit.

This argument is logical and looks a lot like the following mathematical proof:

1. The set of all numbers contains the set of all odd numbers.

2. The number three is an odd number.

3. Therefore, the set of all numbers contains the number three.

But what do you think about Astell's premise that existence is a perfection? It raises some problems. First, it may be better for some things not to have existence—such as the coronavirus. Second, is existence a quality something has, or is it the container for all the qualities something has? Questions along these lines make this premise and other versions of the ontological argument highly controversial.

C. S. Lewis—The Moral Argument

Plato wrote one of the top-10 all-time greatest works of literature: *The Republic*. One of the many masterful passages in this book is a thought experiment about a boy named Gyges, who finds a ring that enables him to become invisible. Plato discussed what Gyges did with the ring and asked his reader: what would *you* do with it?

"I'd get away with murder," some would say to themselves as they giddily fantasize about how they would take whatever they wanted, whenever they wanted, from anyone.

But, on second thought, would they really?

Probably not. Most people have an inner moral voice that prevents them from doing wrong even when no one is watching. Or, if it doesn't prevent them, the moral voice haunts them later. You couldn't stand those sleepless nights, living with the bad person you'd become. You have a conscience.

C. S. Lewis, a 20th-century British philosopher and writer, took the existence of conscience as evidence for the existence of God. The vast majority of human beings all over the planet believe that they ought to try to be good. Why? If we were just the accidental by-product of a random explosion in the cosmos, we would have no reason to judge ourselves. The concept of goodness we use to judge behavior must come from a supreme source of goodness.

Granted, we sometimes disagree about what it means to be good. For example, we may argue over whether it's okay to take a hotel towel. But notice—the very fact that we are arguing over the answer presupposes that there is an answer. Right and wrong exist. The Nazis were wrong. No sane person wants to be like them.

Where does this moral standard come from?

Some argue that morality is a *herd instinct* our species evolved for survival. When parents are kind, their children grow up and reproduce, passing on the family genes. When neighbors are kind, their community defends itself more effectively against enemies, and so on. In this sense, morality is a natural adaptation that has given our species an extraordinary advantage.

Lewis recognized the existence of herd instincts in both humans and animals. He argued, however, that morality cannot itself be a herd instinct because it is often used to judge herd instincts. For example, the Nazis displayed a great deal of herd instinct—working together, protecting each other, fighting for one another. And yet, we condemn them.

So, we are left with a question: is morality a kind of meta-herd instinct, emerging from the trial and error of other herd instincts? If so, then it may not have a divine source after all.

J. L. Mackie–The Problem of Evil

We have just surveyed four of the most influential arguments for the existence of God. You can decide for yourself whether you think any of them work. Even if none of them work, this doesn't disprove God's existence. It could be that God exists even though we cannot prove it.

But J. L. Mackie, a 20th-century Australian philosopher, developed an argument to disprove God's existence. Although Epicurus, whom we will meet later, is credited with inventing this argument, Mackie explained it so clearly that he has become famously associated with it. It is based on the simple question that you may have asked yourself when you were 10 years old: why do bad things happen to good people?

This argument is known as the *problem of evil* (or *suffering*). It would take a very big book to convey the extent of the problem. Let's narrow it down to just one type of evil: child abuse. No, let's narrow it down to just a single case of child abuse: Jenna. There's no need to spell out what happened to Jenna. Suffice it to say, it's really, really bad.

The question is: why? If God exists, then it seems that what happened to Jenna simply should not have happened.

Mackie listed the following three statements:

1. God is omnipotent.

2. God is wholly good.

3. Evil exists.

Someone who believes in God has to agree with all three statements. Yet, Mackie argued, the statements are logically inconsistent, making belief irrational. If God is omnipotent, he can do anything he wants. If he is wholly good, he wants to help Jenna. Yet he doesn't. Jenna's suffering proves there is no God.

The common response to this line of reasoning is known as the *free will defense*. It argues that Mackie's three statements are consistent after all. God wanted to create humans with free will, like him. If you give people the ability to choose, you can't stop them from making bad choices.

Mackie's concern with this response was that it fails to grasp the extent of omnipotence. God could have made humans stronger and smarter so that they never, or rarely, chose evil.

Consider the fact that Jenna's abuser is mentally ill. Is it even accurate to say that this person is freely choosing to abuse Jenna? Now consider how widespread mental illness is. Why would God create so many humans with poor ability to make good choices? A truly omnipotent being could have done so much better.

Will some good come out of Jenna's experience to make her suffering fair and worthwhile? The nonbeliever seriously doubts it. The believer can only hope.

THOUGHT EXPERIMENT
THE INVISIBLE GARDENER

From the 20th-century British philosopher John Wisdom. Once upon a time, two men came to a clearing.

"Look," said the first man. "There are flowers here. Someone is tending this clearing."

"No," said the second man. "Look at all the weeds. This clearing is untended."

But neither man could convince the other. So, they sat down each day to watch. When no gardener was observed, the first man insisted that the gardener must come at night. So, they pitched a tent and watched. When, once again, no gardener was observed, the first man insisted that the gardener must be invisible.

The second man harrumphed. "How is your gardener different from no gardener at all?"

Is God like the invisible gardener? Believers claim he causes many wonderful things in the world. Yet he cannot be observed. The world contains a lot of not-so-wonderful things, like the weeds in the garden. No one thinks you need a gardener to cause weeds. Do you need a gardener to cause the flowers? Do you need a god to cause wonderful things? Why or why not?

CHAPTER THREE

Who Am I?

When you look in the mirror, what do you see? Do you see a physical body composed of nothing but swirling atoms? Or do you see an immaterial soul peering out from behind your eyes?

Science tells us that your body was composed of an entirely different set of cells 10 years ago. In fact, only a small number of brain cells stay with you throughout your life. Are those brain cells enough to make you the same person from beginning to end? You have certainly changed over the years. Does this mean that you have been a succession of different people throughout your life?

Whether you accept metaphysical idealism (only the perfect forms of things are truly real), metaphysical realism (the physical world is truly real), or some combination thereof will affect your conception of yourself. And your conception of yourself will in turn affect the kind of life you choose to live.

Zeno of Citium—Stoicism

Many people today admire stoicism. We use the term *stoic* to describe someone who endures suffering without complaint. This term derives from an ancient school of thought that flourished in the Mediterranean region for about 600 years, before Christianity took over.

Zeno of Citium, a third-century-BCE Greek philosopher, was the founder of Stoicism. He believed that all of reality is physical—composed of matter and *pneuma*, which is life force. Pneuma pervades the cosmos, giving it organization, growth, and motion. Stoics often called pneuma "soul," even though they believed it to be a combination of fire and air and therefore purely physical. For them, the world around us is real, and there is no other spiritual or abstract realm.

However, Zeno believed in God as well. Though he often called God "Zeus," he did not think of God as the thunderbolt-throwing bully his fellow Greeks worshiped. For Zeno, God is pneuma—the life force of the cosmos, the *world soul*. Zeno went as far as perceiving the entire universe as a single, living entity. Everything that exists, including each human being, is a divine fragment of that whole.

To illustrate Zeno's concept of a person, consider a burning log. God is the fire; the log is your body. God is within you, inseparable from you, giving you light and heat. God exists in the world at different levels—it is the force that enables rocks to hold together, plants to grow, animals to move, and humans to think.

Human thought is reason, and reason is the purest expression of divinity. Zeno called it the *Logos*. Logos is the ultimate law of the universe. All things must exist and act in accordance with Logos. The secret to a happy life, according to Zeno, is to accept Logos and not try to fight it.

To illustrate the point, Zeno told a memorable story about a dog tied to a moving cart. If the dog wants to follow the cart, then it will move along with the cart without noticing that it is being pulled. But if the dog does not want to follow the cart, it will be dragged anyway and the dog will be miserable.

Zeno said, "Happiness is a good flow of life," which means that we should strive to conform our will to the Logos. When bad things happen, and you react emotionally, you reduce yourself to the level of an animal, capable of movement but not thought. Reason should enable you to understand that nothing that happens is really bad or good in itself—it is simply what has to be.

The Stoic concept of a person is both humbling and inspiring. You are not the individual you seem to be: as part of the world soul, you are part of God.

Simone de Beauvoir—Existentialism

There could be no more opposite view to Stoicism than existentialism. Existentialism is comparatively new—less than 200 years old—and not a unified school of thought. It has no clear founder. In fact, existentialists tend to deny being existentialists! They do so because the whole idea of existentialism is to be an absolute individual—to define yourself and create your own meaning.

The 20th-century French philosopher Simone de Beauvoir was an important figure in the existentialist movement because of her impact as an early feminist. Her book *The Second Sex*, published in 1949, traced the systematic mistreatment of women throughout history and urged women to break free of sexism. Breaking free requires rejecting God and the many social institutions that continue to give men priority over women.

Beauvoir pointed out that so much of who you are is determined by the society in which you live. Your hairstyle, makeup or facial hair, clothing, shoes, the expression on your face, the thoughts in your head—all of these things are strongly shaped by what you feel is expected of you.

To this, you might respond, "Not true! I choose what I want."

Really? Then put on a clown costume tomorrow instead. Could you go about your day looking and acting "outside the box"? You probably wouldn't want to. What an extraordinary coincidence that "what you want" is *so very similar* to what millions of others in your demographic also happen to want! Clearly, you are "choosing" within a very narrow set of options, strictly defined by society.

Although both men and women face societal expectations, Beauvoir was particularly concerned about women. She famously said, "One is not born, but rather becomes, a woman." By this statement, she meant that there is no biological basis for the feminine behavior and appearance women adopt. Femininity is a social construct, and a bad one, because it makes women look weak and incompetent in comparison to men.

Fortunately, the existentialist universe is not governed by necessity like the Stoic universe. Beauvoir believed we can realize we are living inauthentic lives and become true to ourselves. Authenticity is not a one-time change but a constant challenge. According to Beauvoir, you must self-consciously choose who you are *at every moment*.

The bright side of existentialism is that anything is possible. You are the creator of your own life. The dark side is that you alone will bear the responsibility for what you create.

Daniel Dennett–Reductionism

Daniel Dennett is one of the most prominent American philosophers alive today. He stands firmly by the biological explanations that existentialists reject. His view is called *physical reductionism* because he believes all facts can be reduced to physical facts. In particular, he argued that facts about who we are can most accurately be understood simply as facts about bodies with brains.

For Dennett, the question "Who am I?" is misleading. It suggests that there is something other than our bodies which needs to be identified. In his view, however, there is nothing else. Our idea of a subjective self is an illusion.

Dennett looks to Darwin's theory of evolution to explain the nature of all organisms, including human beings. Our species evolved over millions of years just like other animals, who have no sense of self. Notice that cats never wonder who they are. Cats cannot even recognize themselves in the mirror. Their brains process instinctual responses to the environment without reflecting on that process.

What sets the human brain apart is a powerful adaptation: language. Naming and describing things enables us to assign significance to them. To a cat, this pile of stones is just an obstacle to climb over. To a primitive human, it becomes a sacred altar to an unseen god who will provide protection to its worshipers. Although this is just a story, it has power: it unifies otherwise disconnected and aimless individuals.

Your ability to name and describe yourself works much the same way. It unifies otherwise disconnected and aimless instinctual responses to the environment. When you reflect on your own life history and tell a story about it, you create a self.

For existentialists, the self you create is real because it has the power to choose different goals. For Dennett, the self you create is not real because your goals are already completely determined by your biological makeup. All facts about yourself reduce to facts about your body and brain. So, no matter how much you may think you defined yourself by choosing *this* path rather than *that* path, you did not really have a choice. Still, the story that you did have a choice gives you a sense of significance.

But wait—*who* is telling the story? Don't we need a self in order to tell a story about a self in the first place?

Not according to Dennett. After all, we can program a robot to write a story about itself even though it is nothing but a machine made of metal. Likewise, nature can program us to write stories about ourselves even though we are nothing but machines made of flesh and blood.

David Chalmers—Dualism

Dennett's arch nemesis is David Chalmers, a contemporary Australian philosopher who denies that all the facts about who we are can be reduced to physical facts. Chalmers grants that neuroscience may one day fully explain our brain functioning. Nevertheless, it will never solve the *hard problem of consciousness*: why do we have such rich subjective experiences?

Consider music as an example. What is it?

First of all, music is an event that unlocks a cascade of physical responses in the body. Instruments create sound waves that cause the eardrum to vibrate, which causes ear fluid to move, which causes tiny hairs to bend, which creates electrical pulses, which are transmitted though nerves to the brain—triggering hormones, such as oxytocin, serotonin, dopamine, and endorphins—which flow through your blood, boosting vitality.

But music is also an experience. No matter how accurately detailed, a purely physical description of Beethoven's Symphony No. 5 will always be missing something—namely, *what it's like to listen to it*. Sound can be measured in purely quantitative terms, but music can only be measured qualitatively. This is to say that it cannot really be measured at all. Music elicits a subjective response called *qualia*. The most advanced robots, which can even dance to music, still do not have qualia. They register sound waves; they don't hear music. Chalmers argues that, if we were purely bodies with brains, we could not have qualia either.

We don't just register wavelengths of light, we see *color*. We don't just inhale particulate matter, we smell *fragrance*. Color, fragrance, taste, and music are qualia. Not only do human beings have qualia, but we are also *conscious* that we have qualia. An unconscious person does not experience music. Qualia can only occur in something that is aware.

Is this thing a soul?

Throughout history, philosophers who affirmed the existence of body and soul have been called "dualists" because they posit two kinds of substance—material and immaterial. Chalmers's concern about dualism is that it traditionally conceives the immaterial substance of the soul in supernatural terms: the soul is able to survive the death of the body and live on as some kind of ghost.

Recall that Dennett killed this ghost by reducing the mind to brain only. For Dennett, consciousness is an illusion—it doesn't really exist. Chalmers, in contrast, is a dualist since he posits the mind to be both the brain, which is matter, plus consciousness. Yet Chalmers is a *naturalistic dualist* since he conceives consciousness as a property of matter—it cannot go floating off by itself.

Still, Chalmers faces a big question: how can a purely physical thing like the brain specially produce a nonphysical property like consciousness?

This question, known as the *mind-body problem*, has pushed Chalmers toward the conclusion that human consciousness is not special. Consciousness is a property of all matter—a universal force, like electromagnetism. Though everywhere, consciousness manifests itself in proportion to the complexity of its matter. So, a rock will manifest the least, whereas a human being will manifest the most, with a range of levels in between. The view that consciousness pervades the natural world is known as *panpsychism*.

THOUGHT EXPERIMENT
THE FLOATING MAN

From the 11th-century Persian philosopher Avicenna. Imagine coming into existence as a fully formed adult suspended in the air. You are blindfolded and deprived of all other sensory input. There is nothing to smell, taste, hear, or touch. All you can do is wonder about who you are.

Do you know that you exist? Yes. You are definitely aware of your own thinking, which cannot be nothing.

Do you know that your body exists? No. You are not aware of anything physical.

For Avicenna, this thought experiment vindicates dualism. It suggests that you and your body must be distinct things since you can have knowledge of the one (your mind) without having knowledge of the other (your body). From this it follows that you must have a soul.

CHAPTER FOUR

Am I Free to Make Choices?

As we have seen, the question of who you are rests heavily on whether you are free to make choices, especially in the face of uncontrollable circumstances. Freedom seems to be such a valuable thing. Throughout history, brave men and women have fought and died for political freedom. But do human beings have free will?

Free will is the ability to act according to one's own discretion and without any constraints. So, suppose it is raining and you are deciding whether to go out. In the end, you choose to go out. You have free will only if, with nothing being different, you could have chosen to stay inside instead.

Determinists reject free will. They say that in order for you to have chosen to stay inside, you would have had to be built with a different preference. Meanwhile, indeterminists maintain that free will enables you to act against your preference or with no preference at all.

While the existence of free will may seem obvious, it is actually difficult to prove.

Epicurus–Atomism

The third-century-BCE Greek philosopher Epicurus founded a school of thought that thrived in the Mediterranean region during roughly the same 600-year period as the Stoic school and was its chief rival. Whereas the Stoics taught that the goal of life is to live in harmony with divine reason, indifferent to pleasure and pain, Epicureans taught that the goal of life is to avoid pain and seek higher pleasures, especially those found in friendship.

The disagreement between Stoics and Epicureans begins in cosmology with their contrasting theories of the universe. Rejecting the Stoic view that the entire cosmos is divine, Epicurus quipped that if there are any gods, they must be away on holiday. The cosmos has existed for all eternity and is composed entirely of atoms—tiny, indivisible particles of matter. Epicurus proved the existence of atoms long before the invention of the electron microscope.

There are objects all around you that can be divided into smaller objects, and then divided again. But this process of division cannot go on forever. Therefore, there must be atoms. Furthermore, atoms must be in motion in order to explain how objects move. Atoms could not move if they were packed wall-to-wall like bricks. So, there must be space between them. Epicurus called this space "the void."

Reality consists of atoms moving according to the laws of physics through the void.

If the atoms always moved in parallel lines through the void, they would never collide and we wouldn't see the collections of atoms, which are the objects around us. The existence of objects proves that atoms sometimes swerve in the void. Epicurus apparently conceived of these swerves as random sideways motions that, though tiny, have momentous cumulative effects.

In addition to creating many different life forms, swerving atoms produce free will. They liberate human beings from the necessity of physical laws, allowing us to act in surprising and unpredictable ways. If I choose to go out in the rain, I could have chosen to stay inside instead because the atoms in my brain may have swerved in the opposite direction.

But is this randomness enough to secure free will? After all, the main purpose of free will is to give our actions personal significance. How can I take responsibility for a choice that is random rather than deliberate? Free will must be something we do, not something that happens to us unawares. To make his proposal for free will work, Epicurus owes us an account of how the human brain controls its swerving atoms.

Elizabeth Anscombe—Indeterminism

Elizabeth Anscombe offered Epicurus assistance. A 20th-century British philosopher, Anscombe argued that it is a mistake to suppose everything is either causally predetermined or random. This dichotomy takes the so-called laws of physics too seriously. Perhaps the laws of physics provide a baseline that cannot be violated. They may be enough to explain the behavior of simple objects, such as planets, but they are insufficient to explain the behavior of complex objects like animals and human beings.

Consider a child's card game. We shuffle the cards and deal half to each of us. Then we take turns laying down our cards one by one. The winner is the one who lays down the highest number of red cards.

This is a silly game because the deal determines from the start who will win. There is hardly any point in laying out our cards in turn. Although we may build some suspense from our ignorance of the deal, and we may be surprised by the result, it could never have been otherwise. Even if we suppose a random deal, no one can take responsibility for winning or losing.

If life is like this card game, then all events are predetermined and therefore inevitable. There is no point in getting out of bed in the morning—though we will have to anyway!

In Anscombe's view, life is not like the child's card game but like a game of chess. The laws of physics are the rules of the game. They permit a range of possible moves. But our suspense over who will win is real—it could go either way.

Simple objects, like planets, cannot display the full range of causality the laws of physics permit. They go around and around and around with little variation—much to Isaac Newton's delight. Animals, however, are complex. Although they may not be able to break any physical laws, they can display a much fuller range of causality.

Human beings display a special kind of causality through intentionality. When I act purposefully, I intend to accomplish something through my action (whether or not I am successful). Suppose I grasp a lever and start moving my arm up and down. You ask me why. My answer has nothing to do with atoms or physical laws. My answer concerns my intention: in order to pump water. And what do I further intend by pumping water? To help someone—or to hurt someone? Intentional action is the type of causality needed for moral responsibility.

Epictetus—Divine Determinism

Stoics were deeply concerned about preserving a place in the universe for moral responsibility. One of Stoicism's foremost proponents was a former slave named Epictetus. Following Zeno, the founder of Stoicism, the second-century Turkish philosopher Epictetus affirmed that everything in the universe must obey the Logos, or divine law. This implies determinism: no one can do other than they do. Yet, paradoxically, Stoics insist that human beings can act freely. In fact, Epictetus regards free will as the highest moral achievement for a human being. How can this be?

Consider the Stoic conception of the divine. God is the sum total of reality, which is strictly ordered by the Logos. As the law of the universe, the Logos is necessary. It cannot be other than it is. To wish that it could be otherwise would be like wishing that 2 + 2 = 5. It is impossible.

But this impossibility defines the limit of reality. Without any limit, reality would be sheer chaos. Suppose you are learning to play the harp. All the wrong techniques are a terrible hindrance to you. They create ugly noise. Making beautiful music depends on strictly disciplined adherence to the right technique. Achieving musical excellence occurs only within a precise limit.

Rationality is God's only limit, and its boundaries are what enable him to be maximally excellent. Like a harpist who has internalized the right technique, God has internalized rationality. There is nothing external to God to impose restraints. So, although God cannot do other than he does, he is free.

Notice that this amounts to a different conception of freedom. Rather than conceiving freedom as the ability to do otherwise, as Epicureans do, Stoics define freedom as the ability to act without external restraint. This conception of freedom is known as *compatibilism* because it holds that being determined is compatible with being free.

Epictetus argued that rationality enables human beings to identify with the Logos. More than anything else in nature, we are capable of transcending the material aspect of our nature. Our bodies are external restraints. Like overloaded donkeys, our bodies carry the burden of emotions—fear, anger, sadness, joy—all of which cause us to behave irrationally. To be free, we must focus instead on what is in our control—namely, rational thoughts.

Someone can take you prisoner and enslave your body, but they can never enslave your mind. Epictetus knew this from personal experience. After he was set free from enslavement, he realized that desires about the physical aspect of existence are equally enslaving. Through willpower, we can shed those desires and achieve divine freedom. The secret is to want only what is in our control. Epictetus wrote, "There is only one way to happiness and that is to cease worrying about things which are beyond the power of our will."

Thomas Hobbes—Physical Determinism

The 17th-century English philosopher Thomas Hobbes was concerned about the notion of "willpower" that plays such a pivotal role for so many philosophers. For example, the

Stoics claimed that the entire universe is physical, but then they went on to claim that the human will can transcend the limitations of the human body. Hobbes would insist that they can't have it both ways. If the entire universe is physical, then nothing can transcend physical limits. Alternatively, if the will *can* transcend physical limits, then it is not just physical, making dualism true.

Hobbes came down in favor of physical determinism, against dualism. In his view, the entire universe is material and functions according to physical laws without allowing human beings to achieve the divine freedom Epictetus envisioned. In fact, God plays no role in Hobbes's philosophy. Hobbes probably would have denied the existence of God altogether if he could have done so without landing in trouble.

Hobbes would grant that Epictetus was right to see human beings as beset with physical desires. What Epictetus failed to see is that the strongest desire always wins. There is no rational willpower that can triumph over our desires. Rationality is nothing but the calculations we make to satisfy our strongest desires. If I want an orange more than anything else right now, then I must calculate where and how to get one. My reasoning is the means to the end; my desire is the end.

Hobbes believed that our desires are built into us by nature and are always selfish (even when we pretend otherwise). Our first priority is what we need for survival. Our next priority is what pleases us. Freedom from external constraint is a high priority, since constraints prevent us from satisfying our other desires. However, Hobbes famously argued that it is rational to trade this freedom for safety.

Picture the *state of nature*: a world in which human beings are completely unconstrained. In this world, life would be "nasty, brutish, and short," as Hobbes famously quipped, because we would have to fight constantly to get what we want. In order to avoid such a violent existence, human beings should agree with one another to obey a strong ruler. The resulting security will enable us to get what we want more effectively than we would have when we were completely free. So, in addition to rejecting the existence of free will, Hobbes argued that it is a rational calculation to give up freedom from external constraint in exchange for security.

Jean-Paul Sartre—Existentialism

The 20th-century French philosopher Jean-Paul Sartre agreed with Hobbes about the irrelevance of God. In fact, living in a much more tolerant era, Sartre openly declared himself an atheist. However, he would be critical of Hobbes's mechanical picture of the world. In Sartre's view, by reducing human beings to machines, physical determinism fails to account for our lived experiences.

Consider martyrdom. If human nature is essentially selfish, how do we explain people who knowingly chose to sacrifice their lives for a cause? Being a prisoner of the Nazis during World War II afforded Sartre the opportunity to reflect on questions like this one, which demonstrates the impressive variety of human choices. He came to the conclusion that there is no such thing as human nature. The members of our species may be prone to some common desires, but what we make of them is up to us.

Sartre was the lifelong companion of Simone de Beauvoir, the existential feminist whom we discussed in chapter 3. The pair never married nor had children, resolving to prove that our choices are not determined by societal or biological forces. Sartre argued that we can make our own choices because there is a *nothingness* within us that is open to infinite possibility—free will. Perhaps we can think of Sartre's nothingness along the lines of Epicurus's void. It is the empty space required for striking out in a new direction.

Sartre noted, however, that free will produces anxiety. It is overwhelming—Sartre would even say *nauseating*—to be faced with so many possibilities. So, we are tempted to find ways to ignore and deny our innate freedom.

Consider a waiter in a fine dining restaurant. He wears a uniform that makes him look like all the other waiters. He recites the proper greeting and the menu specials all day long. In the role of the waiter, he cannot choose different clothes or different actions. His job has been determined and assigned to him. All he has to do is follow directions.

Like the waiter, we want someone to figure out our lives for us. It is much easier to follow directions! But this is the cowardly way out, which Sartre called "bad faith." He urged us to reject the safety of playing a predictable role. We should bravely embrace our freedom, pursuing original projects that give meaning to our lives.

Sartre did more than anyone to define and popularize the existentialist movement. Existentialism means that, for human beings, "existence precedes essence." An essence is the indispensable set of qualities that gives something its identity. In most things, essence precedes existence. For example, a rabbit is essentially a rabbit before it lives out its predictable rabbit existence. Human beings, in contrast, "turn up" in the world without an essence and have to become something, creating their own identity by existing as they choose.

Sartre famously said, "Man is nothing else but what he makes of himself." This idea evidently struck a chord. On the day of Sartre's funeral, 200,000 people poured onto the streets of Paris to mourn his death.

THOUGHT EXPERIMENT
THE CALCULATING DEMON

From the 19th-century French philosopher Pierre-Simon Laplace.
Imagine a superintelligent demon who knows the exact position and momentum of every atom in the entire universe. He also knows all the laws of physics. Will he be able to calculate the future?

Pierre-Simon Laplace said yes. Laplace thought his demon would be able to predict everything that will ever happen down to the smallest detail and that he would also be able to retrace the entire history of the universe. However, Laplace was assuming a mechanical universe like the one Dennett and Hobbes envision. Existentialists like Beauvoir and Sartre would insist that free will thwarts Laplace's demon. They were convinced that science does not do justice to human existence. But even a thoroughgoing scientist might quibble with Laplace. For example, quantum physics seems to prove the universe to be inherently indeterministic. What do *you* think?

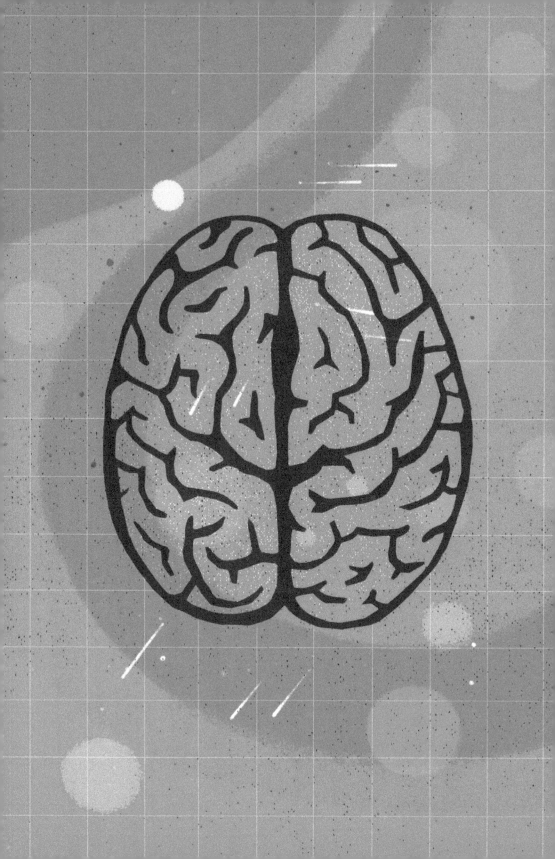

PART TWO

Epistemology

Epistemology is the study of knowledge. It is a very tricky business because it attempts to study how we study, to know how we know.

We view reality through many different lenses. Gender, race, religion, age, nationality, class—these identities affect the way we see the world. We are wearing tinted glasses. Only when we encounter someone whose glasses are tinted differently do we realize it. We also realize that it is very difficult to take our glasses off and that everyone is wearing a pair.

Part of growing up is finding out that your parents view the world not with perfect clarity, but through imperfect lenses. And what about your teachers? The government? The media? Even if they don't deliberately deceive you, they too see the world through filters of their own and might mislead you by accident. The take-home message is alarming: trust no one.

Except yourself. Philosophers reassure us that there is no reason to despair of the possibility of knowledge. We simply have to figure out how to make our own judgments about the truth.

CHAPTER FIVE

Can We Know Anything?

Judging the truth is like any other kind of judging. Suppose you're asked to judge a dance contest. The first thing you'll need is a set of criteria. What matters—audience approval? Originality? Costumes? Performance length? Difficulty of moves? Are certain specific steps required? You get the idea. Once you have a set of criteria, you can rate the competitors.

How do we rate all the different ideas that compete for the title "knowledge"? Unfortunately, the criteria themselves are controversial. Throughout history, philosophers have made a variety of proposals. The following theories are among the most influential.

Zhuang Zhou—Relativism

In the fourth century BCE, the Chinese philosopher Zhuang Zhou proposed a theory of knowledge based on the observation that everything is constantly changing. Yesterday, you looked at the tree outside your window. When you look at it again today, you assume it is the same tree. But this assumption is inaccurate. Today's tree is not the same as yesterday's tree. In fact, this moment's tree is not the same as last moment's tree. Our whole world is constantly in flux.

Is there something beyond the constant change that stays the same? After all, in order for raindrops to disturb the surface of a pond, there must be a surface of the pond to be disturbed. If there were no such surface, no underlying sameness, you would be unable to make sense of the difference the raindrops are causing.

Following the teaching of Laozi, whom we will meet later, Zhuang Zhou was a major proponent of Daoism. The word *Dao* literally means "the way." But Zhuang Zhou also used this word to name the sameness underlying the changing world. This sameness is the cosmic Dao, the source of all being. Daoism is the way to attune ourselves to this absolute principle.

For Zhuang Zhou, however, there is not just one way to be in harmony with the Dao. Different perspectives on the world suggest different ways. Zhuang Zhou was known for expressing his points in the form of parables. He wrote, "You can't discuss the ocean with a well frog—he's limited by the space he lives in. You can't discuss ice with a summer insect—he's bound to a single season." Likewise, the human mind is bound by human concerns, unable to encompass a universal point of view.

Zhuang Zhou teaches us to live with relative truths. The frog can know things about his well, the mosquito can know things about his season, and we can know things about our own world. But even within the human world there are sub-worlds, each with its own knowledge. We must talk to each other to find out about each other's worlds, without presuming that the way of our world will hold for anyone else.

Zhuang Zhou promoted *relativism*, the view that something could be true for one person but not another. For Zhuang Zhou, we cannot hope for a single criterion to judge what counts as knowledge. Realizing, however, that there is an absolute cosmic principle out there, and we should each strive to construct our own knowledge as honestly and attentively as possible.

Sextus Empiricus—Skepticism

Like Zhuang Zhou, the second-century Egyptian philosopher Sextus Empiricus noticed the many differing perspectives among people. Unlike Zhuang Zhou, he was pessimistic about our ability to discuss them peacefully. In his experience, people were always trying to persuade others of the superiority of their own perspective—whether in religion, politics, or philosophy. Doing so causes stress and strife, which detract from the enjoyment of life.

If achieving happiness is our goal, Sextus reasoned, then we should seek neutrality. The fourth-century-BCE philosopher Pyrrho of Elis proposed *skepticism* as the way to accomplish this goal. According to Pyrrho, the wise person is someone who suspends judgment about controversial issues and takes no part in debates about what we can know. Sextus adopted and promoted Pyrrhonian skepticism.

Sextus found the greatest support for this approach in the *problem of the criterion*. Those who claim to be able to judge perspectives must have a criterion for ranking them. But what about this criterion? It has either been judged to be true or not. If it has not been judged, why should we trust it more than any other random criterion? Or, if the criterion has been judged, by what criterion? The same question will arise for that criterion: has it been judged to be true or not? And so on, and so on, to infinity. Therefore, we should not claim to be able to judge perspectives.

Sextus was careful to distinguish Pyrrhonian skepticism from academic skepticism, a rival school of thought defended by the Roman philosopher Cicero. Whereas the former maintains that we cannot know any *perspective* to be true, the latter maintains that we cannot know *anything at all* to be true. So, for example, academic skeptics will claim they cannot know whether there is an elephant in the room.

The problem with academic skepticism is that it would seem to make daily living very difficult. In particular, how will you eat if you don't know what food is? Sextus argued that living life requires a harmless kind of factual knowledge. We can believe whatever directly affects our senses while remaining skeptical of any indirect, theoretical claims. Doing so should naturally bring tranquility, the heart of happiness.

The problem with Pyrrhonian skepticism is that it seems to refute itself. It tells us that we should not judge any perspective to be true. But Pyrrhonian skepticism is itself a perspective. So, it seems Pyrrhonian skepticism tells us we should not judge Pyrrhonian skepticism to be true. Or is there a way out of this self-contradiction?

René Descartes–Rationalism

The 17th-century French philosopher René Descartes saw skepticism as the starting point rather than the final destination. If we begin with the realization that everything we think we know could be wrong, we can build a solid foundation of knowledge.

Descartes made this "method of doubt" famous with a dramatic thought experiment. Imagine that an evil genius is deceiving you about your entire life. Everything you seem to be experiencing right now is an illusion and all your memories are false. You do not know who you are. You do not even know whether you have a body, since the body you seem to have is part of the illusion.

Although this is just an imaginary scenario, it is not impossible, meaning there is no way to prove it wrong. You have to admit that there is a tiny chance it could be true. This tiny chance is enough to show that all Sextus's "harmless factual knowledge" is uncertain, just as the academic skeptics said. Descartes's brilliance was to create this radical state of doubt—and then show us the way out.

Notice that, under the evil genius, you cannot trust your senses. You cannot claim to know anything you see, hear, touch, smell, or taste. But is there anything you *can* know?

Surprisingly, the answer is yes. There is one thing the evil genius cannot deceive you about—namely, your own existence. If you are doubting everything, then there must be a "you" who is doing the doubting. Every time you say to yourself, "I am thinking that my whole life is an illusion," you affirm your own existence as a thinking being.

Descartes summarized his discovery in the formula "I think, therefore I am." Our existence as thinkers is something we can be perfectly certain of—even in the worst-case scenario. For Descartes, this theory proved that reason is more reliable than sensation. Whereas sensation is inescapably prone to illusion, reason can overcome illusion through "clear and distinct ideas." Descartes's view came to be known as *rationalism*, because it depends on logic rather than experience.

Identifying himself as a thinking being was just the first step for Descartes. Using clear and distinct ideas as his criteria for knowledge, Descartes believed he could prove the existence of God and his creation, thereby restoring the world the evil genius had cast into doubt.

John Locke—Empiricism

The 17th-century English philosopher John Locke rejected Descartes's rationalist criteria for knowledge. His primary motivation was to bolster the scientific revolution, which was taking place all around him, most notably thanks to his friend Isaac Newton. Locke worried Descartes's method of doubt undermined the importance of observation in scientific discovery.

Notice that clear and distinct ideas are not objectively observable. What is clear and distinct to one person may be confusing and vague to someone else. Such a subjective criterion for knowledge, Locke charged, runs the risk of enabling bossy people to force their opinions on others.

Rationalists attempted to escape this charge by insisting that clear and distinct ideas are self-evident. This means anyone who reflects on them will necessarily see their truth for themselves.

But Locke countered that, in order for an idea to be self-evident, it would have to be innate, meaning born within us. Only by existing in our minds prior to any experience ("a priori") would an idea be more evident than an idea derived from experience ("a posteriori").

Locke pointed out, however, that God, Descartes's prime example of a clear and distinct idea, cannot be considered innate. First, the idea of God varies considerably from one culture to another. Second, some cultures have no idea of God at all. Surely, if the idea of God were innate, it would be universal.

Against rationalism, Locke boldly asserted that the mind at birth is a *tabula rasa* (blank slate). There are no innate ideas. Any ideas we find ourselves thinking about are derived from experience. This approach, which came to be known as *empiricism*, underscores the importance of experimentation in science.

Because rationalists regard *deductive logic* as clear and distinct, they use it to draw conclusions about the natural world. For example:

1. All gold has five properties: A, B, C, D, and E.

2. This object is gold.

3. Therefore, this object must have property E.

This argument is deductively valid, meaning the conclusion is certain, if the premises are true. According to Locke, however, it ignores the very questions scientists should be investigating. Is this object really gold? Are there different types of gold? Can gold gain and lose certain properties?

For the science lab, Locke recommended *inductive logic*. For example:

1. All the gold we have examined so far has five properties: A, B, C, D, and E.

2. This object has four properties: A, B, C, and D.

3. Therefore, this object is likely to have property E.

The conclusion of an inductive argument is only probable, never perfectly certain. But science doesn't need perfect certainty, according to Locke. His criterion for knowledge is objectively observable evidence—the more the better, even if no amount of evidence can provide a guarantee.

Simone Weil—Mysticism

Descartes and Locke disagreed with each other much like their forerunners, Plato and Aristotle. Whereas Plato and Descartes looked for knowledge within, Aristotle and Locke looked for knowledge in the world. It is worth noting that this disagreement between internal and external orientation is a theme throughout the entire history of Western philosophy. The debate has been productive—each side forcing the other to refine their views with ever greater sophistication.

Although Descartes and Locke disagreed over whether inductive or deductive logic is better suited for the pursuit of knowledge, they were at least united in their allegiance to logic itself, as are most philosophers. Some philosophers, however, rebel against the *logocentrism* of the entire debate.

The 20th-century French philosopher Simone Weil is a good example of this rebellion. Though she began her career strongly interested in Descartes and Plato, she took the notion of God as a perfect, clear, and distinct idea so far that it was no longer just an idea—it was an experience.

Weil was a mystic, meaning that she claimed to have direct personal encounters with God. She did not just believe in God or have faith in his existence; she was certain of it. Weil wrote, "In what concerns divine things, only certainty will do."

There is no doubt that Western logocentrism has led to technological advancement. But what about spiritual advancement? Working as an activist after having lived through WWI and WWII, Weil was deeply concerned that humanity was pursuing the former at the expense of the latter. She pointed out that the ancient Greeks regarded the study of mathematics as a window to the divine. She agreed, not because mathematics is logical—on the contrary, because math reveals knowledge beyond the limits of logic.

Consider the crucial mathematical concept of the square root. A square root is a factor of a number that, when multiplied by itself, gives the original number. For example, 2 is the square root of 4 and 3 is the square root of 9. But what is the square root of 2? It is not any whole number. It is 1.414 . . . an infinite decimal. But an infinite decimal is not a rational number. In fact, the square root of 2 proves that irrational numbers exist.

Likewise, for Weil, the infinite difficulties we encounter in our lives prove God exists. In particular, life produces a constant struggle between necessity and goodness. I need food to survive, but my use of food deprives others of it, which causes suffering. To philosophers like J. L. Mackie, whom we met in chapter 2, such suffering proves that belief in God is irrational. Weil agreed, but embraced irrationality as a legitimate criterion of knowledge. In her view, God is just as irrational *and just as real* as the square root of 2. Suffering reveals the divine mystery.

THOUGHT EXPERIMENT
THE BUTTERFLY DREAM

From the fourth-century-BCE philosopher Zhuang Zhou. Zhuang Zhou famously told of the time he dreamed that he was a butterfly. He flitted around the flowers and forgot that he was Zhuang Zhou. When he woke, he did not know whether he was Zhuang Zhou who had dreamed he was a butterfly, or a butterfly dreaming he was Zhuang Zhou.

Have you ever had such a realistic dream? Is it possible you are dreaming right now? What criteria could you use to prove you aren't?

CHAPTER SIX

What Makes Something True?

Truth is not the same as knowledge. Granted, a belief cannot be knowledge if it is not true. If someone claims to know that Cleopatra existed and we find out this is not true, then we say they did not know it after all. But there could be truths that no one knows. For example, did Cleopatra wear purple underwear? We don't know and it may be impossible to find out. Yet surely, the answer is either yes or no. Therefore, the statement "Cleopatra wore purple underwear" is either true or false.

It seems Cleopatra must have made that statement either true or false by wearing what she wore. But what does it mean to *make a statement true*? When you choose what color underwear to wear, do you cause a truth to exist? Where or in what sense does truth exist? Does a truth exist even if no one knows about it? What is truth?

Nagarjuna—Emptiness

The third-century Indian philosopher Nagarjuna is known as "the second Buddha," next to Siddhartha Gautama, the founder of Buddhism, whom we will meet later. Nagarjuna made the beguiling claim that there is no truth. This claim only makes sense within the context of his interpretation of Buddhism.

Buddhism begins with the observation that human beings are constantly thinking about how we can improve our lives. Ironically, this makes us miserable. A beggar lives under a bridge and all he can think about is how much better it would be to live in a house. So, he toils for a house and soon all he can think about is how much better it would be to live in a palace. Our problem is that we crave things that can only give us temporary satisfaction.

Buddhism teaches that all suffering comes from desiring things that don't last. The only way to escape suffering is to eliminate desire, but this is very difficult. Buddhism offers a variety of suggestions as to how it can be accomplished. Nagarjuna's unique proposal is the *doctrine of emptiness*.

Nagarjuna taught that everything is empty. Even emptiness is empty. What he seems to have meant is that nothing has an enduring essence. Recall from our discussion of Sartre in chapter 4 that an essence is the indispensable set of qualities that gives something its identity.

When you desire a palace, you create a false reality in your mind of a permanent structure that is going to satisfy your desire once and for all. But what is the palace, really? Just a temporary building up and then crumbling down of stone and wood. Likewise, when you desire to be free of pain, you create a false reality in your mind of a thing torturing you. But what is pain, really? Just a rising and falling of sensations. And what are *you*? Just a brief coming together of different elements that eventually disintegrate.

If nothing in the world has an essence, then nothing can be the object of your desire. Every desire requires a permanent object. Because the objects of our desires are all impermanent, we can never be satisfied. Only by letting go of our belief in permanent objects can we let go of our desires.

Of course, if permanent objects do not exist, then we cannot really talk about them. Like desire, words require permanent objects to give them meaning. If everything is in a continual process of transformation, then we can never properly name things or make true statements. If we cannot make true statements, then there is no ultimate truth.

Nagarjuna was content to acknowledge the conventional truths we use to survive. For example: "The sun has risen." "I am cold." "You are here." But from the cosmic perspective, in which everything is constantly transforming, these statements don't even name any identifiable objects, much less count as truths.

So, setting aside conventional truths, the ultimate truth is that there is no truth. Nothing can be named or talked about, not even the nothingness itself.

G. W. Leibniz–Necessity

Unlike Nagarjuna, the 18th-century German philosopher G. W. Leibniz believed in essences. In fact, he believed that our world contains the greatest possible richness and variety of essences. Leibniz argued that we know this because God is a perfect being. A perfect being would create a perfect universe. A perfect universe is one that cannot be improved—neither qualitatively nor quantitatively. God created "the best of all possible worlds."

This thesis may make Leibniz seem insensitive to suffering. His contemporary Voltaire wrote a scathing satire called *Candide* that portrayed Leibniz as "Dr. Pangloss"– a ridiculous optimist who had trouble believing in his own thesis when the world finally beat him down. But Leibniz's thesis is part of an ambitious philosophical system that provides an intriguing account of truth.

Consider the paradigm case of a true statement: "Caesar is Caesar." Who could dispute this? It is a *tautology*. Given that the word *is* designates equality and given that a thing is always equal to itself, the statement is necessarily true. Any variable could be substituted for "Caesar" with the same certainty: A is A, B is B, and so on.

But now move to a harder case of a true statement: "Caesar crossed the Rubicon River." The verb "crossed" does not seem to provide us with a logical way of relating the subject, Caesar, to the object, the Rubicon River. It seems the only way to decide whether the statement is true would be to go back in time, stand on the banks of the river, and see what Caesar does.

But Leibniz cautioned that witnessing a fact cannot make a statement true. What makes it true, according to Leibniz, is what he called the *principle of sufficient reason*: "No fact can hold or be real, and no statement can be true, unless there is a sufficient reason why it is so and not otherwise."

Why did Caesar cross the Rubicon? Given that this is the best of all possible worlds, *he had to*.

According to Leibniz, Caesar has an essence that contains every fact about him. Picture Caesar as an enormous set of facts, which can be expressed mathematically like this:

$$C = \{1, 2, 3, \ldots\}$$

Crossing the Rubicon is just one of those facts, say, number 572. So, to assert that Caesar crossed the Rubicon is to assert that the set C contains number 572. In other words, number 572 is a member of set C:

$$572 \in \{1, 2, 3, \ldots\}$$

This is true and necessary, not because we have witnessed Caesar crossing the Rubicon, but because a world in which Caesar does not cross the Rubicon is not the best of all possible worlds.

For Leibniz, each of us and every other essence in the universe is a special kind of set (which he called a *monad*) containing its sum total of facts, as conceived from God's timeless perspective. Therefore, all truths are necessary. They are guaranteed by the principle of sufficient reason for the best of all possible worlds.

David Hume—Skepticism

Have you ever experienced a principle? What color was it? How did it smell?

No, you've never experienced a principle. You couldn't have. That's because principles are not observable things in the world. They are abstract ideas in our minds.

Leibniz was a rationalist like Descartes. We can tell because Leibniz regarded the principle of sufficient reason as knowledge. An empiricist would not be entitled to regard such a principle as knowledge since empiricists believe all knowledge comes from experience through the five senses.

The 18th-century Scottish philosopher David Hume was an empiricist. Although he wanted to follow Locke's claim that probability can secure knowledge, he noticed a big problem. Probability is based on the logic of induction, but induction is based on a principle that empiricists will have a hard time counting as knowledge!

To illustrate why, let's return to Locke's inductive argument about gold discussed earlier:

1. All the gold we have examined so far has five properties: A, B, C, D, and E.

2. This object has four properties: A, B, C, and D.

3. Therefore, this object is likely to have property E.

What really justifies this inference? Why do we assume that things we have observed in the past are likely to be the same in the future?

The answer is that we believe in an abstract idea, which Hume called the *principle of the uniformity of nature*: the things we have not yet experienced are likely to resemble the things we have already experienced.

It may seem as though you have experienced this principle. Every time you let go of a stone, it falls to the ground. You've tried it a hundred times. Each time is the same.

Surely, this example should count as experiencing the principle of the uniformity of nature?

But it doesn't. It counts as experiencing a stone. That's all. A gray, odorless stone that has, in the past, fallen whenever you let go of it. Look closely at the stone. Does it contain a principle? Of course not. So, it does not have to behave as you expect. The next time you let go of it, the stone might fly into the air instead of falling to the ground.

"But that's impossible!" you object.

A rationalist like Leibniz, who believes in principles that govern the world, has the right to call a flying rock impossible. But an empiricist like Locke does not even have the right to call it improbable because probability is based on the logic of induction, which is based on a rationalist principle. Hume concluded that the *problem of induction* conquers empiricists: empiricists have no empirical justification for their own logic.

This insight shocked great thinkers like Albert Einstein, inspiring him to overthrow Newtonian physics. But Hume didn't let his discovery trouble him. He was content with the Pyrrhonian skepticism of Sextus Empiricus, whom we discussed in chapter 5. Hume recommended that we simply continue to follow our customary beliefs without justifying them.

Ludwig Wittgenstein— Correspondence

It bothered Hume, however, that a lot of customary beliefs are pure nonsense. He found superstition especially troublesome. Suppose someone tells you they observed someone walking on water. Hume asked, "Which is more probable: a miracle or a lie?" Hume thought the lie was more probable, arguing that we should not believe in miracles. But according to his own analysis, which we just examined, probability is just a customary belief. So, he found himself in the awkward position of pitting one customary belief against another.

The 20th-century Austrian philosopher Ludwig Wittgenstein believed empiricists need something more than custom to anchor the truth of statements. He set out to show that a true statement is one which corresponds to facts. This concept may seem obvious, but it is notoriously difficult to explain because connecting a statement to a fact requires an account of how human language comes to represent the world.

Think about it. When you tell your friend, "The lion is attacking the antelope," you cause your friend to think a certain thought. How extraordinary it is that by making a small sound with your mouth (or a few scratches on paper) you can cause something so specific to happen in someone else's brain. How did you do that!?

Wittgenstein proposed that language represents the world in much the same way a picture does. It's not that the sentence "The lion is attacking the antelope" *looks like* a lion attacking an antelope. Rather, the sentence *has the same structure* as what the lion is doing. This is to say that the world consists of things doing things in certain ways. Therefore, our sentences consist of subjects attached to verb phrases with various modifiers.

A lion is not able to talk. His roaring is incomprehensible because it does not mirror the structure of the world. Roaring does not pick out a fact by naming a subject and attaching it to a verb phrase. So, there is no translation. We can translate any language that mirrors the structure of the world—even if it does so in a very different way (such as with characters instead of words). This is because facts provide the meaning. When the structure of a fact corresponds to the structure of a statement, it makes that statement true.

An interesting implication of Wittgenstein's *picture theory* of language is that we can only talk about facts. We cannot talk about religion, morality, art, or philosophy. Statements on these topics are not facts but opinions. Since they do not correspond to any observable structure in the world, they are not meaningful. Wittgenstein was fine with this, famously insisting: "Whereof one cannot speak, thereof one must be silent." He believed the true job of the philosopher is to show people that most of what they talk about is pure nonsense.

Susan Haack—Foundherentism

After publishing his picture theory, Wittgenstein gave up philosophy, since, by his own account, philosophy is nonsense. However, he returned to philosophy later in life with the proposal that language works more like a game than a picture.

Consider the game of Monopoly. We make our moves in accordance with the rules, trying to achieve our goals. I "buy" a "house." This action has no meaning outside the game, of course. The little plastic house does not represent any real house. The little paper money does not represent any real money. The game is a closed system. It makes sense only because the moves are connected by a logical set of rules.

Wittgenstein came to see language this way—it need not correspond to any facts in the world as long as it provides a logical set of rules for interaction. For example, if my goal is to spend time with you, I will use a certain set of words and gestures with you; if my goal is to get away from you, I will use a different set of words and gestures. Each of us uses language to make moves toward our goals.

Some regard the later Wittgenstein's game theory as a replacement for the early Wittgenstein's picture theory. Others, however, regard it as a supplement. Perhaps when we speak of facts, our statements must correspond to the world, and when we speak of opinions or abstract ideas, our statements need only link with each other in a logical way.

The contemporary British philosopher Susan Haack thinks science itself requires a compromise of this sort. After all, any scientific theory will involve some observational statements, such as, "The lion attacked the antelope," along with some abstract statements, such as the principle of the uniformity of nature. We need a theory that admits both fact-based (empiricist) and abstract (rationalist) types of truth.

Haack proposes a new metaphor: Science is like a crossword puzzle. We start with the clues. The clue for 1-across is "Attacker of antelopes." This could be any number of things. But the row for 1-across has four boxes. So, we fill in LION. But the column for 1-down, under the L, has eight boxes. So, "lion" will only work for 1-across if L works as the first letter of 1-down.

For Haack, the crossword puzzle metaphor illustrates how science is a combination of evidence and mutual support. Using the clues to generate possible answers is analogous to finding facts in the world. Using the grid to eliminate possible answers is analogous to applying abstract principles. The facts provide empirical foundations; the principles provide the coherence of logical links.

Since previous epistemological theories, *foundationalism* (correspondence) and *coherentism* (non-correspondence), focused exclusively on one or the other, Haack calls her combined approach *foundherentism*.

THOUGHT EXPERIMENT
THE STOPPED CLOCK

From the 20th-century English philosopher Bertrand Russell. The question, "What makes something true?" is often another way of asking, "What is knowledge?" It is tempting to define knowledge as "true belief." But the following thought experiment challenges this definition.

Suppose you wake up groggy on the couch with the shades drawn. You look at the clock—it says 2:00. So, you believe that it is 2:00. In fact, it really is 2:00. Little do you know, however, that the clock stopped 12 hours ago!

Your belief is true and completely justified. But what made it true? The wrong thing. So, is your belief really true after all? Do you really know that it is 2:00?

CHAPTER SEVEN

Is Science Really Objective?

We live in the age of information. It is so satisfying to learn about empirical research that supports our personal views. "A recent study found that our favorite desserts are actually good for us!" Hmmm . . .

Science aims to be objective, meaning free from bias. But how successfully does it realize this aim? Are we using science to tell us what we want to hear?

There's no doubt that scientists bring biases to the lab. For example, scientists are more likely to research things that are easier to measure. This is called the *streetlight effect* by analogy with the drunk who lost his wallet in the yard but is looking for it on the street because the yard is too dark! It is human nature to be biased.

Though bias is inevitable, can science successfully correct for it? This is a matter of philosophical debate.

William James—Pragmatism

William James trained as a physician and wrote the world's first psychology textbook in addition to becoming a pre-eminent 19th-century American philosopher. As a scientist, he was concerned about minimizing bias, but as a philoso-pher, he invented *pragmatism*, a view that holds there is no such thing as objective truth.

Pragmatism defines truth as belief that proves useful. Beliefs that correspond to facts generally prove useful. Likewise, beliefs that logically link together generally prove useful. So, James was happy to accept the correspondence and the coherence theories discussed earlier. Like Haack, he saw them as complementary. However, his pragmatism went beyond a combination of the two theories. He argued that a belief does not have to correspond or cohere in order for it to prove useful.

James was especially interested in justifying religious belief. Religious beliefs do not correspond to observable facts and they are more mystical than logical. Yet, a reli-gious belief may prove useful to you—giving you hope, inspiring you to be good, or uniting you with other believers. If so, then it is true for you. Conversely, if religious belief is not useful to you, then it is not true for you. The truth can be different for different people.

James did not mean to limit pragmatism to religion—he meant to apply it to all areas of life, including science. Truth is not a set of statements written in stone but the process by which each of us "marries new experience with previous experience."

For example, James investigated a woman who claimed to be able to speak to the dead. When he attended her séances, he had to marry these experiences to his previous experiences with frauds and with genuinely spiritual people. For many years, he believed her claim was true, but in the end decided it was false.

Pragmatists do not say that truth is whatever you *want* it to be. This would be unchecked bias—a dishonest and dangerous mindset. We must diligently look for evidence for or against a claim before believing it, because we know that, in the long run, it is useless to ignore the facts. But when the evidence is inconclusive, and the claim is useful, we have the right to believe—which is the same as judging the claim to be true for us. Good pragmatists know that such a judgment is never final. They are always open to revising their beliefs in light of new experience.

Karl Popper—Falsification

The 20th-century Austrian philosopher Karl Popper argued that science enables us to come much closer to the ideal of objectivity than pragmatists believe. He promoted the scientific method kids now learn at school, which we can summarize as follows:

Step 1: Identify a problem or puzzling observation.

Why are all the swans in Australia black?

Step 2: Generate a possible explanation.

Snow is rare in Australia and the waters are dark with tannin. Swans are colored black for camouflage.

Step 3: Test the explanation.

All the swans in snowy regions should be white.

You might think that the way to conduct the test is to seek confirmation of the explanation that all the swans in snowy regions will be white. But Popper rejected confirmation for three reasons. First, it would be impossible to check all the swans in snowy regions. Second, even if you did, it wouldn't prove that black swans *couldn't* live in snowy regions. Third, seeking confirmation will feed your natural biases—you'll tend to see what you want to see.

Instead of seeking confirmation, you should seek falsification. Hunt for black swans in snowy regions—better yet, invite rival scientists to start the hunt. If one is found, then we have a counterexample, which proves your theory false. If none are found, however, your theory stands.

According to Popper, a theory that is *falsifiable* but yet *unfalsified* is science at its best. Conversely, a theory that is not falsifiable is not even science.

For example, Popper argued that Sigmund Freud's theory of psychoanalysis is not science. Suppose a man named Albert comes to Freud feeling depressed. Albert tells Freud he dreamed of shooting his cousin. According to Freud's theory of psychoanalysis, dreams reveal subconscious sexual desires. So, Freud explains Albert's depression is the result of a suppressed desire to have sex with his cousin.

If he is a scientist rather than just a storyteller, Freud needs to test his explanation. But what does his theory predict? It is not clear. Suppose it predicts that Albert will feel better if he talks to his cousin, but doing so actually makes him feel worse. Although his failed prediction should count as falsification, the vagueness of psychoanalysis makes it easy to interpret that negative reaction as confirmation of the suppressed desire instead. In fact, Freud boasted that psychoanalysis could explain any human behavior—even the most surprising. Hence, Freud's theory is not falsifiable.

Scientific theories, in contrast, make specific predictions that can be disproven. For example, we might propose that

Albert suffers from a vitamin D deficiency. This explanation yields the prediction that taking a vitamin D supplement will make Albert feel better. If Albert takes vitamin D and feels no better or even worse, then we must go back to the drawing board for a new theory.

Predictions are risky, meaning that they might fail. But this is good, in Popper's view. By risking failure, we work against our biases. Scientists may never achieve pure objectivity, but they can come close through trial and error.

Thomas Kuhn—Paradigms

Twentieth-century American philosopher Thomas Kuhn became convinced that Popper's portrayal of how science works is inaccurate. Popper pictured scientists making observations that falsified previous theories, prompting them to propose new theories. Kuhn argued, however, that scientists were far more likely to ignore or explain away problematic observations.

For example, suppose you find a black swan in the Arctic. You could maintain the camouflage hypothesis by explaining the black swan as the result of some additional factor, such as random mutation or global warming. Alternatively, suppose you give up the camouflage hypothesis in favor of the hypothesis that Australian swans need dark melanin to protect their skin against the burning Australian sun. Still, both camouflage and melanin are hypotheses of adaptation within the theory of evolution. No scientist would see the black swan as a challenge to the theory of evolution itself. Scientists will be united in their determination to find some evolutionary explanation, thereby confirming, not falsifying, their shared theoretical framework.

Kuhn called scientists' shared theoretical framework a *paradigm*. He argued that scientific inquiry normally consists of scientists quibbling over issues that arise within their paradigm. Like Haack, he compared science to a crossword puzzle but emphasizing its limitation: you can't work off the grid.

Kuhn further noticed, however, that there are crisis moments in history when the grid itself is overturned. For example, in the 16th century everyone believed the Earth was the center of the universe. Astronomers were busy proposing ever more elaborate hypotheses to explain why the path of planets across the night sky looked so irregular. Then along came Nicolaus Copernicus, who realized that what we see in the night sky makes a lot more sense if the sun is the center of the universe. Copernicus's revolutionary new conception of the solar system was not welcome. But with the help of other brave individuals, it slowly caused a paradigm shift in astronomy.

To appreciate how disruptive this shift was, imagine that your Arctic black swan is just the first in a series of anomalies that become so glaring that the theory of evolution itself must be rejected, making way for a new paradigm that makes perfect sense of all the anomalies.

The theory of evolution falsified?! For most biologists, such a possibility would be very hard to imagine. And maybe it will never happen. But it would a mistake to think that our current theories must be correct. If we could travel 500 years into the future, we would be amazed by how many of our paradigms had shifted by then.

Kuhn's vision of history is startling. Since each paradigm provides its own standard of knowledge, all truth is relative to a paradigm. We see judgments as "rational" or "well-supported by evidence" from within a paradigm.

There can be no absolute standard of truth outside of all the paradigms through which the paradigms can be compared. Scientific claims can be called "objective" only within their own paradigm, not within the grand scheme of things.

Michel Foucault—Power

The 20th-century French philosopher Michel Foucault agreed with Kuhn that the objectivity of any scientific claim is relative to the theoretical framework in which the claim is made. Calling the theoretical framework "discourse" rather than "paradigm," Foucault made some disturbing observations about the nature of science.

Consider the fact that, in the Middle Ages, people who acted up in public were thought to be possessed by supernatural forces. If they said the right things, then they were revered as prophets of God. If they said the wrong things, then they were spurned as witches or demons.

Today, people who act up in public are thought to be mentally ill. They are taken to a doctor, diagnosed, treated, monitored, and cared for.

You may think this shows that our society has made such great progress in humanitarian decency. But don't be so sure. According to Foucault, medieval religion and modern science are just two different discourses. There is no meta-discourse from which to pronounce the one better than the other. In fact, both discourses are equally driven by the lust for power, which have had negative consequences for disenfranchised groups.

Imagine a prison where inmates are locked in cells that are fully visible to a guard in a tower. Although the guard does not watch all the inmates at all times, he *can* watch any of them at any time. The inmates know about the guard and they cannot see one another. The 18th-century philosopher Jeremy Bentham envisioned such a prison and called it *the panopticon*.

The panopticon is an ingenious method of control. Without knowing when they are being watched, the inmates are forced to internalize the expectations of the guard. Completely exposed, without any privacy or freedom, they come to guard themselves.

Foucault argued that modern science has created an invisible panopticon for us. We are the subjects of invasive studies, surveys, and surveillance. Although we are not observed constantly, we never know when we are being observed, and so we internalize the expectations of the observers.

Foucault was particularly concerned about sexuality. No scientist follows us into the bedroom. Yet studies we see in the media serve to judge us as though they did. "Sixty-Three Percent of Women Have Rape Fantasies," "Human Beings Are Naturally Bisexual," "Pornography Is Linked to Divorce." We internalize the labels, categories, disorders, and health standards that scientists dream up, enabling science to control us.

Taking Foucault as a starting point, feminist philosophers like Helen Longino, Linda Alcoff, and Lorraine Code have developed a variety of epistemological theories that draw attention to how white male conceptions of knowledge have subjugated women and people of color throughout history. They present an alternative discourse, in the hope that not all discourses need to be driven by the lust for power as Foucault presumed.

Logical Fallacies

The 19th-century American philosopher Charles Sanders Peirce, who was also a scientist and a logician, wrote, "Each chief step in science has been a lesson in logic."

Logic is the study of reasoning. In addition to modeling good reasoning, logicians analyze bad reasoning. Instances of bad reasoning are called *fallacies*. Like a science, fallacy analysis aims to be objective. However, it also involves some debatably subjective elements.

Formal fallacies can be mathematically proven. There are many kinds. Consider the following example:

1. All fish have scales.

2. That creature has scales.

3. Therefore, that creature is a fish.

Although the inference may look fine at first, the conclusion does not follow from the given premises, as can be shown in a diagram:

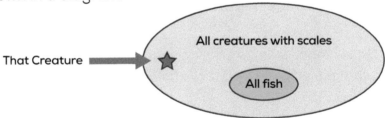

The diagram shows that a creature could be a member of the set of creatures with scales while not being a member of the set of fish. The mistake is an indisputable matter of mathematical fact.

Informal fallacies, in contrast, cannot be mathematically proven. The following is a list of the most common informal fallacies:

Ad populum: The appeal to popularity. "Millions of people all around the world believe in God. So, God must exist."

Ad hominem: The appeal to personal characteristics. "Wittgenstein was a crank. So, I refuse to take his philosophy seriously."

Ad ignorantiam: The appeal to missing information. "No one has proven that the soul does not exist. So, I'm going to assume that it does."

Ad verecundiam: The appeal to authority. "Aquinas is a doctor of the Catholic church. So, I believe him when he says human beings have free will."

Tu quoque: The appeal to hypocrisy. "I may have ridiculed Augustine's arguments, but Augustine ridiculed people's arguments, too."

Hasty generalization: Drawing a conclusion from too small a sample. "I had to study Heidegger's philosophy and it didn't make any sense. So, now I stay away from philosophy."

Straw man: Oversimplifying your opponent's view. "James's whole theory boils down to believing whatever you want."

Post hoc: Taking "X followed Y" to mean "X caused Y." "Marriage must be a bad institution. Whenever people get married, they fight more."

False dilemma: Presenting an artificially limited choice. "Either I am capable of achieving nirvana or my life is meaningless."

Cherry picking: Using a favorite bit of evidence to confirm a bias. "I just found a study from 1975 that shows philosophers' brains are bigger than average."

Begging the question: Using something too similar to your conclusion as your reason. "I prefer idealism because I like it best."

Judging informal fallacies may depend on the context. Usually, the kinds of considerations raised in the aforementioned examples will be irrelevant to the argument. But not always. For instance, it is sometimes relevant to appeal to popularity, as in: we should order pizza, since that's what almost everybody wants.

You'll often see fallacies committed in politics, when disputants become passionate on an issue. But scientists and philosophers have to watch out for the same mistakes in reasoning. Logic is a systematic way of investigating fallacies.

THOUGHT EXPERIMENT
THE QUANTUM CAT

From the 20th-century Austrian-Irish physicist Erwin Schrödinger.
According to quantum physics, particles can exist in an indeterminate state until they interact with other particles. For example, a quantum physicist might assert the following *quantum statement*:

Particle X is indeterminate between "S" and "not-S" until it interacts with particle Y.

This all sounds fine when speaking abstractly, but once we fill in the variables with normal objects, it sounds far-fetched. Let X = a cat, let S = alive, let not-S = not-alive, and let Y be you. Now the quantum statement becomes:

A cat is indeterminate between alive and not-alive until it interacts with you.

What?!

Erwin Schrödinger asked us to imagine a closed box containing a cat and a bomb rigged with a random detonator, so that it is indeterminate whether or not the bomb has detonated. By analogy with the quantum statement, the cat is neither alive nor not-alive until you open the box to look, at which point a determination is made, one way or the other.

Schrödinger used this thought experiment to show that the original quantum statement is absurd. In his view, if this kind of indeterminacy cannot happen with normal objects, then it cannot happen with quantum particles.

Others, however, draw the opposite conclusion. If this kind of indeterminacy can happen with quantum particles, then it can happen with normal objects.

After all, how do you know whether anything at all is determinate one way or the other until you interact with it? For example, how do you know the refrigerator light goes off when you shut the refrigerator door? Does your observation of reality (as a form of interaction) affect that reality? If so, how can science ever be objective?

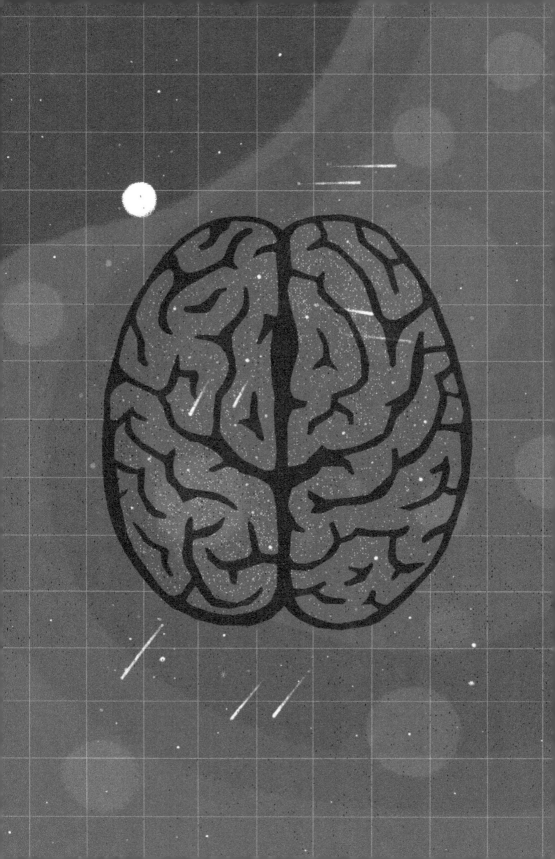

PART THREE

Axiology

Axiology is the branch of philosophy concerned with theories about value. It subdivides into ethics, the study of the good life, and aesthetics, the study of art. Life and art are mirror images of each other. As the old question goes—does art imitate life or does life imitate art?

Philosophers are looking for beauty in both.

Think of your life as a large canvas on which you are painting. What do you want to see there? Although you cannot erase what you have already painted, you can transform unfortunate splotches into the background of a truly inspired foreground. What if you woke each morning ready to add to a growing masterpiece?

Conversely, think of your favorite characters in books or movies. Why do you like them? Do they serve as positive role models? Can your appreciation for a fictional person improve your own character in real life? Thinking about other possible lives adds depth to our own lives. What if the fictional characters you have read about are actually real people reading about you? What would you want to teach them about life?

The philosophers in the following chapters have some compelling suggestions.

CHAPTER EIGHT

What Makes a Good Life?

We live in an age of diversity. No one these days expects there to be a single model for a good human life. Respecting diversity, however, should not prevent us from making judgments. In fact, the diversity of possible life paths we see around us prompts us to consider more than ever before what path would be best for us.

You have about 80 years to live—if you're lucky. What are you going to do with it?

People push along, getting caught up in various pursuits, without questioning the value of their life as a whole. But then there are those moments—in the middle of a sleepless night, at a funeral, or during a time of crisis—when the question looms large.

Suppose you arrive at the last hour of your life with the opportunity to reflect on all the things you did and didn't do. Nothing could be more important than to be able to look back and say, "I lived a good life."

Don't put off the question if you have the opportunity to consider it now: what makes a good life?

Laozi—Harmony with Nature

Take a walk in a park. Watch the sunset color the sky. Inhale the fresh air. Stop and smell the roses. Read some haiku or pastoral poetry.

Does nature do something for you? So many people find their most satisfying moments communing with the great outdoors. Is it just because our species evolved out there long ago? Or is nature still the secret to human thriving?

In the sixth century BCE, Chinese philosopher Laozi defined the good life in terms of harmony with nature. Laozi means "Old Master," and it is not clear that any such person ever actually existed. Nevertheless, he is the legendary founder of Daoism, which we examined in chapter 5 in connection with Zhuang Zhao. The founding work of Daoism, the *Daodejing*, is ascribed to Laozi and often called by his name.

Daoism was born in China during a time of constant war between seven rival states. So, it's unsurprising that Laozi teaches the importance of relinquishing ambition in order to secure peace. But for Daoists, nonviolence is more than just a political solution—it is a way of life.

Laozi emphasized *wu wei*, a concept difficult to translate. It expresses noninterference or nonaction, which entails following the natural course of the universe. When we make a habit of spending time outdoors, we gain a sense of the rhythm of the day and of the seasons. As part of nature, human beings have this rhythm within us. We should not fight it by conforming to artificial schedules, rules, and laws. We should surrender to the eternal force of nature, the cosmic Dao, which flows through us and all things. Laozi wrote, "A good traveler has no fixed plans, and is not intent on arriving."

Although most of the authors discussed in this book were intellectuals, happiest while studying, and convinced that the good life requires diligent learning, Laozi is an exception. After all, formal education requires ambition; it involves taming animal instincts in order to advance civilization. Laozi saw civilization as a corrosive influence. In his view, it is better to cultivate simplicity and empathy for one's fellow creatures than to debate ever more complicated theories of the world.

Daoism is closely associated with tai chi, a form of group exercise ideally practiced outdoors. Tai chi transformed the martial art of combat into the performance of graceful movements and deep breathing for relaxation and inner peace.

Harmony with nature is a mindset that may become increasingly relevant as the world's environmental crisis builds. Laozi's approach provides a spiritual basis for sound ecological practices. It is hard to picture a good life on a barren planet.

Siddhartha Gautama–Detachment

The fifth- to fourth-century-BCE Indian philosopher Siddhartha Gautama was the founder of Buddhism, which we discussed in chapter 6 in connection with Nagarjuna. Gautama would disagree with Laozi that nature is the secret of the good life. The legend of Gautama's personal history explains why.

Gautama was born a prince and raised in a palace. As a young man, he married and had a son. All this while, his father, the king, sheltered him from the outside world. One day, however, Gautama left the palace. He saw four things that transformed him: an old man, a sick man, a dead man, and an ascetic man. In seeing the first three, Gautama realized that his life in the palace was a lie. No amount of wealth or power can prevent the ravages of physical existence. The conditions of nature inevitably cause suffering.

Seeing the ascetic man inspired Gautama to seek an escape from physical existence. Gautama left his family to journey far and wide, slowly gaining wisdom until he finally achieved enlightenment. Gautama accepted the traditional Indian belief in reincarnation we discussed in chapter 1, where physical death does not mean escape from physical existence because it is naturally followed by rebirth into another physical life. Gautama conceived enlightenment as *nirvana*, a final release from this cycle, so that he would not have to be reborn. He came to be called the Buddha, meaning "the enlightened one."

Rejecting elitist conceptions of religion common in his day, Gautama taught that enlightenment is possible for anyone who follows the *Eightfold Path*. The Eightfold Path specifies the right approach to eight dimensions of human life: belief, attitude, speech, action, work, effort, mindset, and concentration. Although the right approach is interpreted in different ways, the common theme is that, in everything we do, we must strive to detach from our physical desires. Gautama said that, just like beads of water that rest on a lotus leaf without adhering to it, the wise do not adhere to the seen, the heard, or the sensed.

All human beings have desires—they cannot be completely eliminated. For example, we naturally want food, and we have to eat to live. However, we can learn to detach from the *desire* for food, so that this desire does not enslave us. Consider that we all know how distracting a sudden craving for sweets can be. Hedonists, who are bent on enjoying sensual pleasures, can quickly become addicted to their desires, resulting in unnecessary suffering. Buddhists, in contrast, practice meditation in an effort to avoid the allure of the physical world and thereby avoid suffering.

Hildegard of Bingen—Enthusiasm

Notice that there is no god in Buddhism. In the West, in contrast, belief in God was officially required until the 20th century. Disbelief in God was equated with disbelief in morality. Hence atheists were regarded as a bad people who were dangerous to society.

Of course, any limitation on freedom of thought or speech runs contrary to philosophy, which searches for the truth wherever it may be found. In fact, we have to credit philosophers throughout history for persistently promoting the intellectual diversity we enjoy in Western countries today.

Under mandatory Christianity, Western philosophers dealt with God in a number of ways. Some were secret atheists, paying lip service when necessary. Some were agnostic—quietly suggesting that no one knows for sure. Others were sincere believers. Among the believers, some cast God as a useful hypothesis that could help explain puzzling aspects of the world. Others were enthusiastic worshippers.

The 12th-century German philosopher Hildegard of Bingen was an extraordinary example of the last category.

The 10th child in a minor noble family, she escaped the burden of medieval motherhood by becoming a nun. After learning to read and write at the monastery, she was soon elected head mistress. Hildegard went on to found new monasteries, to preach on tour against corruption in the church, to publish books about medicine and botany, and to do many other things that were rare for anyone at that time, especially a woman.

Though Hildegard suffered from chronic headaches, she evidently made the most of life. Her secret was the ecstatic inspiration she found in music. Having learned to play the zither as a girl, she began composing when she was in her 40s. Her music was a sensation and is still enjoyed today.

Hildegard saw music as divine and she saw the divine in everything. "So sing!" she wrote. "Be not lax in celebrating. Be not lazy in the festive service of God. Be ablaze with enthusiasm. Let us live as a burning offering before the altar of God." Wow—how many of us have ever been so excited to face the day?

Hildegard was neither the first nor the last philosopher to argue that music has a very central role to play in the good life. (Examples within this book include Confucius, Aristotle, and Nietzsche.) Even if it turns out that music and God aren't for everyone, Hildegard seems to be making a deeper point about the crucial importance of enthusiasm. Perhaps there is something ecstatically inspiring out there for each of us, something that can turn a dreary or painful life into something truly good.

Albert Camus—Sensual Pleasure

The 20th-century French-Algerian philosopher Albert Camus was the exact opposite of Hildegard of Bingen.

Not only did he reject the existence of God, but he also expressed open hostility toward the religious impulse. The problem with religion, Camus argued, is that it promotes hope—the idea that we can survive the present life by looking forward to a bright future after death.

For Camus, hope is a terrible lie. All human life ends in oblivion. There is no heaven, nirvana, or cosmic Dao to look forward to. All our efforts—the songs we write, the temples we build, the solutions we devise—are absolutely meaningless.

Nevertheless, it is still possible to live a good life, according to Camus. The secret is to admit that death is the ultimate reality and then resolve to live anyway.

Camus famously used the myth of Sisyphus to illustrate his view. Sisyphus was a king who angered the gods. For punishment, they forced him to spend all day pushing a heavy boulder up a mountain. When he reached the top, the gods sent the boulder back to the bottom so that he would have to push it back up again the next day. Sisyphus was condemned to perform a pointless task over and over again forever.

For Camus, human life is a Sisyphean punishment. Each day we face the problems of work and relationships. We toil to exhaustion, only to face much of the same again tomorrow. Our lives are repetitive and unrewarding. We cannot help wanting the universe to be orderly and meaningful, but when we contemplate the big picture, nothing adds up. The only rational solution is suicide.

"Should I kill myself or have a cup of coffee?" Camus quipped. He courageously rejected the rational solution, embracing absurdity instead. We have the option of accepting our fate with a sense of humor rather than resignation. Camus cultivated cheerful indifference by turning away from the big picture toward *hedonism*, the view that the Buddha rejected—the good life is found in sensual pleasure.

Camus loved to spend long, lazy afternoons at the beach. Picture a blue sky, warm sand, salty breeze, humming crickets, delicate seashells, colorful umbrellas, laughter, bicycles on the boardwalk, a doughnut stand, a coffee shop, and a pub with someone you love.

Maybe you don't have a beach. Maybe all you have is a cup of coffee. Still, it is possible to enjoy a glorious present moment. It is small. It will disappear. But you don't need to think about that. Learn to savor the here and now whenever you can. In Camus's view, this is all the eternity you need.

Camus casts each of us as Sisyphus—a heroic king tragically tortured by the gods. Does this epic self-image appeal to you? Apparently, it hit home, since Camus won the 1957 Nobel Prize for literature.

Alain de Botton—Emotional Intelligence

Take a moment to consider why we see Sisyphus in the mirror. Perhaps it's because we have an overinflated image of ourselves.

The contemporary Swiss-British philosopher Alain de Botton is deeply concerned that heroic portraits of human potential have set our expectations too high. Unrealistically high expectations are reinforced by social media and pop culture in general. If you judge yourself against a superstar fantasy, you're bound to be disappointed by reality.

De Botton recommends a dose of humility. Rather than aiming for an amazing life and failing, how about aiming for a life that isn't bad?

According to de Botton, we face two main sources of trouble—work and relationships. Our work should give us an outlet for our most passionate talents in a way that is appreciated by others and fairly compensated. Yet, we often strive for a career we would rather not have just to earn more money and achieve a higher status. Likewise, the most important thing in a relationship is to be accepted for who we are. Yet marriage, the paradigm relationship in our society, asks us to play so many roles. We must be considerate domestic partners, self-sacrificing parents, reliable breadwinners, exciting lovers, and more, all in one. This is a recipe for disaster.

The secret, for de Botton, is to realize that we do not need to be superstars. Ordinary lives can be good lives, provided they are lived with emotional intelligence.

Everyone has emotional needs. Some are universal, such as the need for love, whereas others are quite idiosyncratic and often stem from childhood. For example, some people need security whereas others need freedom; some need tidiness whereas others need mystery, and so on. We are often unaware of these contrasting emotional needs and how they can lead to conflict.

Emotional intelligence is the solution. The first step is to understand your own emotional needs. The second step is to be able to communicate them to others. The third step is to understand that others have emotional needs, too. Being aware of people's feelings can prevent problematic behavior at work and in relationships.

De Botton jokes that, in an emotionally intelligent society, when two people meet, the standard greeting will be "My crazy is _____. How are you crazy?" Though emotional intelligence may never eliminate the anger, fear, and sadness that torment the world, it can reduce negative feelings enough to make an ordinary life worth living.

THOUGHT EXPERIMENT
THE EXPERIENCE MACHINE

From the 20th-century American philosopher Robert Nozick. Suppose virtual reality technology advances to the point of producing a machine that simulates ideal experiences. All you have to do is tell the machine your tastes and preferences. It will produce a whole new life for you, maximizing pleasure and minimizing pain. You can specify the environment, the people, and your own identity. The machine will set you up with whatever types of adventures you would enjoy. (For the purpose of this thought experiment, don't worry about whether the machine might be dangerous.)

The machine is a dream come true. The only catch is that you can't just try it for a day. You have to choose: stay in your real life or spend the rest of your life in the machine.

It looks like Camus would go for it. But Robert Nozick says he would choose to stay in his imperfect life on the grounds that human beings want to actually do things, not just experience what it's like to do things. What would you do, and why?

CHAPTER NINE

How Do I Decide What's Right?

No doubt a big part of the good life is making moral choices. Fortunately, much of morality is pretty simple: just try your best to be nice! You don't need to be a philosopher to get that.

However, more difficult moral choices do come up regularly. Sometimes they are big choices, like whether to have an abortion. Sometimes they are small choices. But even the smallest moral choices add up and contribute to your character—for better or for worse.

Suppose, for example, someone gives you a gift of a hat that you don't like. Should you show your honest reaction? Or should you pretend to like it?

This small choice demonstrates a conflict between two values—truth and happiness. Most everyone will agree that both are important, and oftentimes we can have both. Although it would be ideal to always have both, life presents circumstances where we have to choose. Are you going to be the kind of person who values truth over happiness or happiness over truth? This is a significant question, and there are many others like it.

A philosopher needs a consistent way to judge moral choices. The following are some of history's most influential theories for deciding what is right.

Augustine—Divine Command Theory

The oldest and most widespread approach to ethics comes through religion. In fact, some people wonder why there is such a thing as philosophical ethics when people are supposed to learn right and wrong at their temple, mosque, or church.

Philosophers feel that, even if religion does teach ethics, we still need a neutral ground for discussing ethics in secular contexts—such as work or school—which include people of widely different religious perspectives. Plus, there is a growing number of people who prefer not to affiliate with any religion. They need ethics, too.

Divine command theory defines morality in terms of obedience to God. Although this approach can be used very narrowly within a particular religion, it can also provide the basis for a religiously neutral ethical theory.

In the fifth century, Roman North African philosopher Augustine developed an argument for divine command theory based on Plato's idealism. Recall that Plato was concerned about the imperfection of the physical world.

Nothing we see around us is perfectly equal, beautiful, or good, and yet we have ideas of perfection. Since
these ideas must have come from somewhere, there
must be another realm beyond the physical world—the
world of forms. Plato saw the world of forms as the source
of all truth.

Being a Christian, Augustine identified the world of forms
with the mind of God. Because God is perfect, he knows
all perfect ideas, and creates the world based on them.
Just as Plato conceived the world of forms as the most
proper object of contemplation, Augustine conceived God
as the most proper object of love. Loving God is equivalent to loving truth—it orders your thoughts and provides
moral guidance.

Augustine felt that immorality arises from loving the
wrong things. It's okay to love things other than God, but
only in proportion as they are worthy of love. For example,
someone who loves sweets too much will choose to eat
them too often, thereby damaging their bodies. Even worse,
someone who loves alcohol too much will soon be unable
to make any good choices. Augustine wrote, "My love is my
weight; wherever I go, my love brings me there."

For Augustine, loving God will generally mean obeying
religious authority, but notice that it could mean disobeying,
if you believe that religious authority is wrong. After all, God
is the highest authority and is able to speak to you directly,
through conscience. No doubt many religious reformers,
such as Martin Luther, justified their disobedience to religious authority in this way. Even further, many philosophers,
such as the American transcendentalists, came to see conscience itself as divine. For them, divine command theory
means obeying your own conscience, even if the rest of
society thinks you're wrong.

Jean-Jacques Rousseau–Social Contract Theory

If the gods ever appeared before us and gave orders directly, we would all be happy to obey. But they never do. Instead, believers have to consult religious authorities, holy books, and ultimately conscience, which can be doubted.

For example, the American transcendentalist Henry David Thoreau famously made a stand against slavery, arguing that conscience called for civil disobedience to the US government. He went to jail for refusing to pay his taxes in July 1846. Thoreau's best friend and fellow transcendentalist Ralph Waldo Emerson, however, was of a different mind. His conscience called him to pay Thoreau's taxes for him and spring him out of jail. Thoreau was not pleased, and the two philosophers argued over the morality of civil disobedience.

Conscience is highly subjective. Is there a more objective basis for ethics?

The 18th-century French philosopher Jean-Jacques Rousseau felt that the evils of civilization have so corrupted individual judgment that conscience alone is no longer sufficient for judging right and wrong. Instead, he proposed social contract theory, which defines morality in terms of an unspoken agreement to unite for the common good.

Imagine the state of nature, prior to the rise of civilization. What would life be like there? As discussed in chapter 4, Thomas Hobbes believed that life in the state of nature would be nasty, brutish, and short. Rousseau completely disagreed. In Rousseau's view, human beings are naturally endowed with pity, an innate aversion to see our fellow humans suffer. In a primitive world where there is plenty of food and shelter for everyone, we would all get along just fine.

Problems arise, however, when population growth depletes resources, causing competition. In this situation, our self-interest would begin to outweigh our pity for others. Worse yet, competition results in winners and losers, with the winners amassing property and leisure time while the losers do all the labor. In other words, social classes are born. Such inequality would soon erupt in a war of all against all, like the one Hobbes envisioned, if we did not establish a political system.

Rousseau famously observed, "Man is born free, but he is everywhere in chains." This is because property owners have established a political system designed to preserve their own wealth. Within this system, it is almost impossible to live a moral life—all our choices are warped by inequality. For example, if we buy new shoes, we contribute to oppressive factory conditions. If we don't buy new shoes, the economy slumps. But this system is not inevitable. Although we cannot go back to the state of nature, we can make an unspoken agreement with one another to unite for the common good.

The political system Rousseau envisioned was direct democracy—everyone voting on everything, without elected representatives. Although this system would be impossible to realize in a nation as large as the United States, it is still possible to practice social-contract ethics. For example, we could resolve not to buy shoes from oppressive factories. Notice that it will not help for just one person to make this resolve. For Rousseau, morality requires mutual agreement. When we make choices, we must conceive of ourselves as acting, not as human individuals, but as agents of humanity.

Immanuel Kant–Deontology

Rousseau's social contract is a beautiful thing. Like a marriage contract, it is meant to create a standard, public expectation. Unfortunately, Rousseau's social contract is also completely imaginary. Since no one ever really signs any documents, ethics becomes a purely theoretical agreement. There is no way to prevent violation of the agreement and no way to force people to "sign" in the first place.

The 18th-century German philosopher Immanuel Kant was convinced that ethics is much more binding than Rousseau thought. When we tell children, "You should be honest," we don't mean they might want to be honest, we mean they *must* be honest. Where does this necessity come from? For Kant, moral necessity comes from the rules of reason. Rationality produces morally sound choices in the same way it produces mathematically correct calculations, such as $2 + 2 = 4$.

How can this be? Surely, there are some highly intelligent but dishonest people out there. Picture an ingenious scammer who takes out a series of loans and then disappears on the other side of the world for a life of stolen luxury. We might not admire this man, but would we call his choice irrational?

Kant would. In Kant's view, anyone who makes a *lying promise* has made a terrible mistake of reasoning. Every time rational agents act, they act on a general principle. For example, when you go to get a drink of water, you are acting on the general principle, "If you are thirsty, then you should drink water." The scammer's principle is: "If you want money, then you should make a lying promise." Although your water principle and the scammer's principle seem equally rational at first, we find an important difference.

The water principle is *universalizable*, meaning that no contradiction arises if everyone drinks water when thirsty. Since human beings are equal, any principle that serves one of us should equally well serve all of us. This is to say that you should be able to universalize any principle you act on.

But the scammer's principle is not universalizable. A contradiction arises when everyone makes lying promises—namely, no one believes in promises anymore because everyone knows that everyone else is making lying promises!

Kant saw choosing to make a lying promise as equivalent to asserting that 2 + 2 = 5. Your choice doesn't add up because you are presupposing the validity of promising while at the same time undermining the validity of promising. Kant further believed that this sort of analysis is applicable to all immoral choices. Being moral is part of what it means to be a fully rational agent. Kant's ethical theory is called *deontology*, which means "duty theory," because it defines morality in terms of obedience to the rules of reason.

John Stuart Mill—Utilitarianism

By securing the necessity of moral choice, deontology also makes morality rigid. For example, since lying promises are irrational, they can never be okay, according to a deontologist. Yet it is easy to imagine a situation where a lying promise might be called for.

Imagine the year is 1944 and you are in Amsterdam hiding a Jewish family in your attic. Nazis come to the door with guns. Promising to take the Nazis to the hiding place, you take them to the basement instead, in order to give the Jewish family time to escape.

This seems like a moral choice—heroic, even. Yet Kant forbids it. A lying promise or any lying is always wrong, in his view, even if the truth has terrible consequences. Deontologists are not concerned about consequences. They contend that morality is a matter of following the rules.

The 19th-century English philosopher John Stuart Mill took the opposite approach. In his view, moral agents absolutely need to calculate the consequences of their choices, following rules only to the extent that they are likely to promote the desired result.

What is the desired result of morality? Utility, Mill asserted, by which he meant as much happiness as possible for as many people as possible. Mill was careful to distinguish his view from religious ethics that regard happiness in heaven as the future reward for morality. He defined happiness as pleasure and the absence of pain in this life. But Mill was equally concerned to distinguish utilitarianism from hedonism, the view that the good life is found in sensual pleasure, which Albert Camus believed. Mill argued for a hierarchy of pleasures, where intellectual pursuits, such as poetry, produce more genuine happiness in the long run than sensual pursuits, such as smoking.

As a young man, Mill was jailed for circulating pamphlets about birth control, which he and his fellow radicals believed would help alleviate the rampant poverty in London. Mill was later elected member of Parliament in the British Government. All his life, he had his eye on practical ways of improving the human condition. His ethical theory can be thought of as a useful guide for those who see themselves as social reformers, as he did.

Utilitarianism defines morality in terms of the greatest good for the greatest number. Notice, however, that the consequences of our actions depend on luck and other circumstances beyond our control. For example, suppose the Jewish family you were trying to help decided to hide in the basement instead of the attic, because they thought the Nazis would look for them in the attic. Then your lying promise did more harm than good. But it would be a shame to blame you for a faulty calculation. Some argue we need an ethical theory that recognizes your courage—even though you both broke the rules (against deontology) and caused terrible consequences (against utilitarianism).

Rosalind Hursthouse—Virtue Ethics

Virtue ethics defines morality in terms of excellent character.

The ancient philosopher Aristotle, whom we met in chapter 1, put courage first on his list of virtues, which also included self-control, honor, charisma, generosity, pride, patience, compassion, honesty, wit, modesty, and fairness. Different lists of virtues are associated with different authors, cultures, and religious traditions. Although they sometimes disagree, they often overlap and provide a promising basis for morality.

Aristotle wrote, "We are what we repeatedly do. Excellence, then, is not an act, but a habit." By this he seems to have meant that we can't judge people's choices apart from their character. To be moral, we have to practice making good choices over the course of a lifetime.

If we don't obey rules or calculate consequences, how do we know what constitutes a good choice?

According to virtue ethics, we need to follow the example of others who have achieved excellent character. Although there is no single formula or prescription for excellence of character, we know it when we see it, as is often the case with complex skills. The contemporary New Zealand philosopher Rosalind Hursthouse argues that practicing virtue ethics is like learning how to cook from an accomplished chef.

Suppose you want to learn to make an omelet. A recipe with instructions is better than nothing. But apprenticing with a master is better than any recipe. Put on an apron and observe her in action. How did she flip the omelet without breaking it? What gave her the sudden idea of adding a pinch of oregano? There is no concrete way to answer such questions. The chef will just shrug and smile. Furthermore, there is more than one master chef. Each one makes omelets a little differently. Watch and learn. As you begin to try their techniques, you'll make some mistakes. Through increasing success, however, you'll find your own style.

Hursthouse's cooking metaphor suggests that virtue ethics conceives morality along the lines of an art rather than a science. Aristotle's style of morality was moderation—he recommended always aiming for the "golden mean" between two extremes of action. For example, courage is in the middle ground between cowardice and rashness. But what constitutes the golden mean in a given situation is a matter of interpretation.

Whereas deontology is a rational science, because it relies on logic, utilitarianism is an empirical science, because it requires predicting results. Each of these approaches has a claim to objectivity lacking in divine command theory. Virtue ethics, in resembling art rather than science, returns to subjectivity in a new way.

THOUGHT EXPERIMENT
THE RUNAWAY TROLLEY

From the 20th-century English philosopher Philippa Foot. Suppose you are standing in the control tower at a trolley station. Looking down from the window, you see that five people are tied to one of the tracks, with a trolley headed straight for them. Although you can't stop the trolley in time, you can switch it to a sidetrack. Just as you reach for the lever, however, you see that there is someone tied to the sidetrack as well.

If you do nothing, five people die. If you pull the lever, one person dies. What should you do?

Based on their philosophical principles, Mill and Kant give opposite answers. Mill would pull the lever, since five deaths is five times less pleasure and five times more pain than one death. Kant would not pull the lever, since pulling the lever violates the moral rule against killing innocent people. What would you do, and why?

CHAPTER TEN

What Do I Owe to the World?

The take-a-penny, leave-a-penny tray on the counter at the checkout is symbolic of morality on this planet— an anonymous exchange of need and generosity between strangers who will never meet.

During your lifetime you will use an extraordinary quantity of resources. For example, according to *The Washington Post,* Americans eat an average of 46 slices of pizza per year. That's 23 pounds of dough, cheese, sauce, and meat every 365 days for your pizza-eating pleasure alone. The world has apparently given you a great deal. Are you going to give something back?

Some people think of their career as a way of serving the world—for example, doctors, teachers, and recycling companies do a lot of good. Others view raising a healthy and kindhearted family as their way to give back to the world.

But where does their sense of obligation come from? Some would argue that it is inaccurate to see good things that come our way as anonymous gifts. Even if the world or its inhabitants have left "spare change" for us, it doesn't follow that we must give something in return.

Philosophers throughout history have offered various suggestions about what, if anything, we owe the world.

Confucius—Inner Propriety

Confucius wrote, "To put the world in order, we must first put the nation in order; to put the nation in order, we must first put the family in order; to put the family in order, we must first cultivate our personal life; we must first set our hearts right."

Confucius lived in fifth-century-BCE China, where one's whole life was shaped by ritual. A ritual is a solemn ceremony consisting of a series of actions performed in a strict order, often with the use of special objects. Although rituals can be expensive and time-consuming, it is hard to think of a better way to make a moment meaningful.

Like most ancient societies, the Chinese practiced rituals for birth, death, coming of age, and other major moments, but they went much further, with rituals for good luck and honoring ancestors. Participation in these rituals required elaborate preparation, from sacrificing an animal to pulling a tooth. Although there is much less patience for ritual in popular culture today, even the most cynical among us still long for meaningful moments.

Confucius accepted the traditional rituals of his culture. His innovation was to emphasize that the most important part of a ritual is not what shows on the outside but what is happening on the inside. Ritual is an opportunity to think good thoughts about the people and events in our lives. He believed that the more we meditate upon good thoughts, the better the world will be. For him, the performance of a ritual was a form of meditation.

Ritual is not something one chooses to do on a whim—it is an obligation. When his mother died, Confucius mourned her death for three years. Confucius valued the respect, thought, and joy encapsulated in ritual so much that he seemed to see life itself as an extended ritual. The way you do your laundry, the way you greet someone on the street, the way you govern a country—all of these things should be respectful, thoughtful, and joyful in the same way as a ritual.

Confucius became a great teacher, with students of all social classes from all across China. Like Aristotle and Rosalind Hursthouse, Confucius promoted virtue ethics, focusing on five main virtues: benevolence, righteousness, propriety, wisdom, and fidelity. Propriety (*li* in Chinese) is the commitment to ritual that is so distinctive to Confucius, and it is what binds the five virtues together in obligation. We owe it to the world to set our hearts right.

Søren Kierkegaard—Radical Faith

Although the 19th-century Danish philosopher Søren Kierkegaard would agree with Confucius that our first priority should be to set our hearts right, he would reject Confucius's commitment to propriety. Kierkegaard argued that there are three stages on the way to a responsible life, and the final stage requires abandoning propriety in favor of radical devotion to God.

Kierkegaard called the first stage *aesthetic*. This stage, common among youth, is devoted to sensual pleasures.

It recalls Albert Camus's hedonism, which we discussed in chapter 8. As a poet, Kierkegaard would always feel strongly drawn to beautiful sights and sounds, tastes and pleasures. However, he insisted that maturity prohibits us from lingering in this stage.

Kierkegaard called the second stage *ethical*. This is the stage in which an adult starts a career and a family, becoming a conventional contributor to society. Ready to settle down as a good citizen, Kierkegaard himself trained to be a pastor and asked a young woman to marry him. Confucius would have approved. Kierkegaard suddenly broke off the engagement, however, when he decided that propriety was just a way of hiding from our highest calling.

Kierkegaard called this third and highest stage *religious*. True religion does not just mean going to church each week and praying each night, which is proper to the ethical stage of life. True religion means becoming a *knight of faith*, someone who is willing to live an unconventional life, doing things society regards as improper or even unethical, in the service of God.

Kierkegaard used the example of Abraham from the Old Testament to illustrate the knight of faith. God called Abraham to kill his son. Abraham was ready to obey, and would have, if God had not sent an angel of mercy to stop him in the nick of time. For Kierkegaard, this Bible story illustrates how someone who loves God with all his heart is willing to forsake any obligation to the world.

Kierkegaard argued that passion for God is irrational, requiring a "leap of faith" and unquestioning devotion. This argument makes him a divine command theorist, like Augustine, whom we met in chapter 9. According to Augustine, if God created us from nothing, then we owe everything to him. Moreover, there is no objective way to justify this religious commitment.

Echoing Augustine, Kierkegaard famously claimed "truth is subjectivity," perhaps meaning that each person has to become their own justification. Kierkegaard is regarded as the grandfather of existentialism because he stressed the radical freedom of the choice to walk away from a normal, respectable life in order to carve out an authentic path that others are not likely to understand or appreciate.

Ayn Rand–Rational Egoism

Kierkegaard had a strong sense of himself as a man with a destiny. Choosing the life of a philosopher, he became infamous in his own day for his critique of conventional morality. He knew his work would live on after his death, making an impact on the world.

This is just the kind of person Ayn Rand admired. Her only quibble would be that Kierkegaard was deluded in using God as an excuse for his artistic genius. In her view, God does not exist. We do not owe him or the world anything and our only obligation is to ourselves.

Rand grew up in Saint Petersburg, Russia, during the Russian Revolution and Russian Civil War. When the communists took over, her father's business was confiscated, leaving her family in abject poverty. Despite these setbacks, Rand managed to earn a university degree by age 19. As soon as she saw her chance, she immigrated to America to become a writer.

Rand despised the communist ideal of an *altruistic society*, where everyone supposedly lives for one another as equals. Her experience taught her that human beings are animals built with the desire to survive and succeed.

All of our rational activity is driven by self-interest, even if we pretend it's not. Any selfless behavior we might display is irrational. Furthermore, because selfless behavior undermines our own survival and success, it is immoral. For Rand, selfishness is not an unfortunate fact that we should work against; selfishness is a virtue.

Rand promoted capitalism because she saw it as the ideal system for promoting selfishness. The heroes of her philosophical novels are people, like herself, who fed their artistic genius and stopped at nothing to share it with the world. Rand's books have sold in record-breaking millions. She shared her talent, not because she owed it to anyone, but because it served her own ambition to become a great writer.

Rand granted that others benefit from the selfishness of talented individuals. In fact, this is how her ideal capitalist society works. By nature, some people will have greater talent than others. Those with greater talent will naturally produce a surplus of goods, which become available to others, so that everyone who makes an effort can achieve happiness for themselves.

Rand's view, called *rational egoism* from the Latin word *ego*, meaning "I," has been widely criticized for presenting an ugly and inaccurate picture of humanity. Even supposing Rand was correct that human beings are built with a strong survival instinct, does this preclude all forms of altruism?

Peter Singer—Effective Altruism

Recall utilitarianism, which we discussed in chapter 9 in connection with John Stuart Mill. According to this view, what matters for morality are the consequences of our actions: we must try to promote the greatest good for the greatest number. So, utilitarians are altruistic, but they always include themselves in their calculations.

Peter Singer is a present-day Australian utilitarian hard at work on big moral problems. Consider the staggering fact that 25,000 people, including 10,000 children, die every day from hunger and related causes (United Nations). Singer does not just shrug sadly at this problem, like most of us. He argues that we could solve it in a short time, if everyone gave a significant portion of their extra income to effective charity organizations, like he does.

Singer is quick to point out that donating money does not just help the needy—it helps the donor. Altruism provides a meaningful form of fulfillment for people, acting as an antidote for the depression and anxiety that increasingly plagues our culture. Singer reports that he and other people he works with on charity projects have experienced the uplifting effect of making a difference in the world. His proposal, *effective altruism*, suggests that kindness and generosity do not need to be self-sacrificing. In other words, you don't have to lose in order to let others win. You can both win.

But Singer is not only concerned about humans. Utilitarianism requires maximizing happiness, which can be defined in terms of pleasure and the absence of pain, or perhaps preference. Notice that nonhuman animals experience pleasure and pain and have preferences. They must therefore be included when we calculate the consequences of our actions. Although a juicy hamburger may give you pleasure, the cow it came from would rather not have spent his entire life in the miserable conditions of a factory farm.

Singer, himself a vegan, argues that it is morally wrong to discount any creature's preference, regardless of species. He popularized the term *speciesism*, parallel to the terms "racism" and "sexism," to name the bias our society has against animals. The preference of animals should be just as important to us as human preferences, according to Singer.

Singer's focus on preference has controversial implications. For example, there are thousands of people in hospitals around the world with severe, irreversible brain damage. If they have no preferences and are using resources that could help people who are suffering, Singer asserts that their lives should be ended. In a similar vein, Singer supports euthanasia to end the suffering of terminally ill patients, if they prefer.

Without demanding self-sacrifice, Singer asks us to reconsider many of our behaviors and assumptions in order to solve big moral problems in the world.

THOUGHT EXPERIMENT
THE INHOSPITABLE HOSPITAL

From the 20th-century English philosopher Philippa Foot. Suppose you are head surgeon at a hospital in which five patients are waiting for new organs. Two need a kidney, two need a lung, and one needs a heart. If they do not receive these organs today, they will die. A healthy young man comes to the hospital with a broken toe. You ask him if he will sacrifice himself so that your five patients can live. He declines. Should you kill him and take his organs anyway?

Notice that this situation is parallel to the Runaway Trolley problem considered in chapter 9. Would you have chosen to switch the track so that just one person would die instead of five? If so, then it seems that consistency requires you to kill the healthy young man to save your transplant patients. Or are there other factors to consider?

CHAPTER ELEVEN

What Makes a Society Just?

Sometimes people think justice is the same as the law. For example, when considering the Inhospitable Hospital in chapter 10, someone might say, "Well, it's illegal to kill people for their organs, so there is no point in considering it." But philosophers aren't interested in what the law *is*, they're interested in what the law *should be*. And it's a good thing, too, because sometimes laws are unjust.

For example, just 170 years ago, slavery was legal in the United States, and it was illegal to help people escape slavery. Any person providing food or shelter to a fugitive slave could be subject to six months in prison and a large fine (about $40,000 in present-day value). Thank goodness brave people, notably including transcendentalist philosophers such as Henry David Thoreau and, eventually, Ralph Waldo Emerson, saw that the Fugitive Slave Act was unjust and disobeyed it.

Would a law allowing surgeons to kill people for their organs be unjust? What exactly makes it unjust? This is a philosophical question. We need to be able to think about the justice or injustice of possible laws. Even more important, we need to be able to think about the justice or injustice of our current laws. What laws are we supporting right now that we will be ashamed of in years to come? What makes a society just? Philosophers have been investigating this question and offer a range of interesting answers to consider.

Abu Nasr Al-Farabi—Hierarchy

In chapter 1 we met Plato, who wrote the all-time number-one philosophy book, *The Republic*. It defines justice as proper ordering. A person is just when the rational part of their soul rules the irrational part. Likewise, a society is just when educated people rule the uneducated.

Plato is actually a little more specific—he asserts that philosophers should be kings. Only someone who really loves wisdom can be trusted with such an important responsibility as ruling. To be great, rulers must have justice in their own souls and also understand how best to structure society.

Unfortunately, because the uneducated members of society don't understand justice, they will be unable to recognize great rulers and disinclined to obey them. So, Plato introduced a concept that would come to haunt Western civilization up to the present day: the noble lie. The philosopher-kings will need to win the obedience of the uneducated people with a symbolic story.

Plato proposed the *myth of the metals*. According to it, God made all human beings out of the Earth, while mixing different metals into their souls—gold for philosophers, silver for soldiers, brass for farmers, and iron for craftsmen. The story is meant to convey that society must be structured in a *hierarchy* where everyone has a natural place.

The 10th-century Persian philosopher Abu Nasr Al-Farabi was deeply moved by Plato's vision of justice. He worried, however, that the myth of the metals was too weak to keep society in order. In his view, only a full-blown religion would be strong enough to work. This meant replacing Plato's philosopher-kings with philosopher-prophets.

In Al-Farabi's ideal society, religion serves as a *similitude* of philosophy. The philosopher-prophet, who has studied the sciences, translates true wisdom into religious metaphor. Believing the religious metaphor as the truth, uneducated people will be content to realize their purpose in life by serving the hierarchy.

In Al-Farabi's view, the purpose of every human being is to achieve intellectual excellence. However, some people are born with greater intellectual ability than others. Whereas philosophers pursue intellectual excellence directly, soldiers, farmers, and craftsmen pursue it indirectly by contributing vital services to a well-ordered society.

Al-Farabi used an analogy to make his case. The brain is the most excellent organ in the body. But the heart, stomach, and lungs all need to perform their function in order for the brain to function. All the parts of the human body must work together to achieve human excellence. Whereas the brain achieves this excellence directly, the other organs achieve it indirectly, through their supportive role. The body was a widespread analogy for a just society throughout the ancient and medieval periods.

John Rawls–Fairness

Unfortunately, Al-Farabi's Platonic theory of justice neglects one crucial point: power corrupts. Even a true lover of wisdom won't stay just for long in the role of a philosopher-prophet with a noble lie the size of a religion in his pocket. History has proven again and again that hierarchy turns to tyranny. There is no way to avoid the need for checks and balances.

Since ancient times, the world has moved steadily toward democracy, which separates the state from religion and shares out the power. Of course, power-sharing does not automatically prevent injustice. In fact, we've seen great injustices—such as classism, sexism, and racism—woven into the fabric of democratic societies.

The 20th-century American philosopher John Rawls set himself to the task of defining justice within a democratic society. How might we unite to support a single political structure despite the diversity of worldviews that a democracy allows?

Rawls took as his starting point the social contract theory we traced through Jean-Jacques Rousseau in chapter 9. Imagine you are living in the state of nature prior to any political order. What government could you and your fellow society members agree to under those conditions? This theoretical agreement would legitimate the resulting government.

The problem is that the state of nature is hard to imagine—as indicated by the fact that Hobbes and Rousseau completely disagreed about what it would be like. Since we can't settle the question of whether human beings are innately selfish (Hobbes) or innately cooperative (Rousseau), Rawls introduced a brilliant new thought experiment to serve as the *original position* for establishing a social contract.

Suppose you and the members of your society come to the negotiation table to vote on what your government will be. The danger is that any accidental majority will win—for example, if the majority are white, male, and rich, they are likely to win the vote for a government that favors white, male, rich people. So, Rawls proposed that we come to the table wearing an imaginary *veil of ignorance.*

Under the veil of ignorance, you don't know your race, gender, class, religion, age, sexual orientation, or any other demographic information about yourself. This ignorance prevents you from bias as you negotiate with your fellow society members, who also wear veils. You won't vote for a government that favors group X, because you don't know whether you will be a member of that group or not. You'll vote for a government that doesn't favor anyone—in other words, a government that's fair.

Rawls thought everyone wearing the veil of ignorance would agree to two principles: equal rights and equal opportunities. He famously defined justice as fairness in this way.

Rawls was in the middle between two extremes. On the one hand, he rejected any kind of hierarchy based on natural inequality or divine right, as we saw in Al-Farabi. On the other hand, he did not think we need to overthrow democracy in order to achieve equality. Rawls was a political liberal. But some philosophers argue that liberalism is not strong enough to eradicate systematic injustices such as classism, racism, and sexism. Let's have a look at three radical approaches to these problems.

Karl Marx—Economic Equality

The 19th-century German philosopher Karl Marx was concerned about economic inequality. It broke his heart to see some people living in the lap of luxury while others struggled to find enough food to survive another day. In his assessment, capitalism was to blame.

Capitalism is the political system that allows business owners to control the buying and selling of goods for personal profit. The idea behind capitalism was to give people incentive to contribute to society by enabling them to earn money producing things people need. For example, suppose you observe that people don't like getting wet in the rain and they also find umbrellas cumbersome to carry. So, you invent and market a new kind of rain hat. If people like it, they will buy it and make you rich.

The problem with capitalism is that it thrives on competition. By presenting a product better than the umbrella, you elbow the umbrella-makers out of business. Likewise, someone else is waiting in the wings with a better or cheaper rain hat, to elbow you out. So, you must find a way to make the best product possible as cheaply as possible.

The easiest way to compete in the capitalist system, and sometimes the only way, is to underpay your employees, leaving them poor. They can't demand higher wages, because there are plenty of unemployed people you can hire to replace them. So, your employees are trapped on a boring production line with barely a living wage, while you endure the stress of keeping your business afloat. Marx argued that, although capitalism seems to benefit the wealthy and punish the poor, it actually makes life miserable for both classes.

Marx's alternative is a communist utopia that banishes competition in favor of cooperation. If you have the idea for a great new rain hat, you can design and produce it as an artisan. Since there is no money to earn in this system, you will share your hats for the love of hat-making, not for the love of riches. Being in control of your own creative production eliminates the boredom of mindlessly producing other people's products, as well as the stress of constantly battling competitors.

Although Marx wanted communism to function without any government, historical experiments with the communist system, such as in the USSR, have usually relied on a strong government to enforce cooperation. The fact that these governments have been subject to corruption and failure does not prevent many people from continuing to value Marx's cooperative vision of justice.

One example is the contemporary Slovenian philosopher Slavoj Žižek. He joins Marx in calling for a *proletarian revolution*, where the working class overthrows the bourgeois class who own the majority of the wealth and property. Žižek argues that this revolution can be achieved only by dismantling the liberal democracy that supports capitalism.

Martin Luther King Jr.– Racial Equality

Whereas Žižek follows Marx in embracing violence as a legitimate vehicle for radical change, other philosopher-activists, such as Martin Luther King Jr., advocate a radically peaceful approach. King was the leader of the American civil rights movement and recipient of the 1964 Nobel Peace Prize. As a Christian minister, he drew much of his pacifism from the Bible, as is well-known. It is not as well-known, however, that King was also influenced by existentialist philosophy.

Recall from chapter 10 that the existential philosopher Søren Kierkegaard stressed the radical freedom of the choice to walk away from a normal, respectable life in order to carve out an authentic path that others may not understand or appreciate. King needed the courage of Kierkegaard's knight of faith in order to protest racial discrimination. He was jailed nearly 30 times, sometimes for trumped-up charges, such as driving 30 miles per hour in a 25-miles-per-hour zone. Although King found understanding and appreciation among his followers, he was widely despised among white Americans, as evident from the 1956 bombing of his home and his ultimate assassination in 1968.

Given the level of bias against Black people in the American South even to this day, violence must have seemed to many like the only way to overthrow systemic oppression. Yet King argued against it for several reasons. From a spiritual point of view, suffering at the hands of the enemy can be redemptive. From a practical point of view, violent methods don't work as well as peaceful methods. Most important, from a philosophical point of view, the ends don't justify the means. As King stressed in his 1963 "I Have a Dream" speech, the end goal of the civil rights movement was brotherly love between the races. But violent means presuppose hatred, not love. King's nonviolence took the form of civil disobedience, inspired by transcendentalist philosopher Henry David Thoreau, whom we met in chapter 9.

One of King's most prominent present-day followers is the contemporary American philosopher Cornel West (b. 1953). West supports King's nonviolent conception of justice to such an extent that he finds America's liberal democracy unacceptably violent. For example, when President Barack Obama received the 2009 Nobel Peace Prize, he spoke against pacifism, citing the need for American military action in the Middle East. Although West had originally supported Obama's presidency, he was deeply disappointed by this compromise, holding out for a more radically peaceful conception of worldwide justice.

Martha Nussbaum—Gender Equality

Like Cornel West, the contemporary American philosopher Martha Nussbaum (b. 1947) has extended her reach to worldwide justice. We live in a globally interconnected community—it is no longer possible to focus on American society in isolation. Nussbaum has been actively involved in international feminist politics, working toward the goal of gender equality.

Recall from chapter 3 that Zeno of Citium introduced the Stoic conception of the cosmos as a world soul, meaning that the entire universe is a single, living entity. Later Stoic philosophers developed this metaphysical picture into a social philosophy, according to which human beings are responsible for one another because we are living one life together. The Stoic philosopher Epictetus, whom we met in chapter 4, wrote that when someone asks you where you're from, you should not reply with your home city or country, you should say, "I am a citizen of the world."

The Stoic social philosophy became known as *cosmopolitanism* from "cosmos" meaning "universe" and "polis," meaning "city." When you conceive of the universe as your hometown, how does this change your conception of justice?

Nussbaum, who regards her position as "neo-Stoic," suggests that we should care about all living beings, including animals, as well as nature as a whole. This goes beyond Stoicism, which limited its scope to humanity. Nussbaum also nuances the Stoic indifference to pleasure and pain, contending that intelligent emotions are a crucial part of caring. For example, anger is a reasonable response to injustice insofar as it contains a condemnation of evil, but not insofar as it contains an expectation of payback. Citizens of the world should treat anger as a transitional state to be replaced by strength and dignity.

Although Nussbaum works primarily within the liberal political tradition, when it comes to addressing injustices toward women, she embraces a more radical approach. Behind closed doors, often in the privacy of their homes, women around the world face torture in the form of rape and other domestic abuse. Liberal democracy condemns torture and stands up to it when it is publicly visible. However, liberal democracy also upholds privacy as a fundamental right—people ought to be able to live their private lives as they wish, so long as they are not bothering anyone else. The result is that women who have the ability to make their plight public can be helped, whereas those who are not able to do so remain beyond the reach of justice. Nussbaum endorses the analysis of radical feminist legal scholar and activist Catharine MacKinnon, who argues that the liberal state may be a hopelessly male-biased form of government that we need to leave behind in order to achieve justice for all.

THOUGHT EXPERIMENT
THE UNCONSCIOUS VIOLINIST

From the 20th-century American philosopher Judith Jarvis Thomson. Suppose you wake up one morning to find yourself attached with intravenous tubes to a famous violinist. He is unconscious and sick with kidney poisoning. You have been kidnapped to help him because you alone have the right blood type. He must be attached to you for nine months. After that, he will once again be able to make beautiful music for the world. If you detach him before then, however, he will die.

The question is: does the violinist have a right to life?

Thomson said no. The violinist has the right to live by means of his own body, but not by means of yours. Thomson argued that the same reasoning applies to a fetus. She therefore concluded that justice requires abortion to be legal.

What would you do about the unconscious violinist, and why? If you can unplug from the violinist, should women be able to "unplug" from fetuses by having abortions? Is there a relevant difference between the two cases, or are they sufficiently parallel to be treated the same way?

CHAPTER TWELVE

What Is Beauty?

Philosophers classically recognize four big values: truth, goodness, justice, and beauty. We have already looked at truth (in epistemology), goodness (in ethics), and justice (in political theory). One prominent theme in our discussion of all three was objectivity versus subjectivity. That is, do these values exist in the world independent of any human judgment or are they human concepts imposed on the world? The philosophers explored in this book are divided on this issue, giving compelling arguments on both sides.

When it comes to beauty, most people these days are inclined to assume subjectivity wins hands down. As the saying goes, "beauty is in the eye of the beholder." But don't be so sure. The following experts on beauty give us plenty of reason to wonder whether beauty isn't just as real as anything else we experience in this world.

Plotinus—Perfection

We often hear people say that beauty consists in symmetry. Dozens of empirical studies claim to show that people judge a face or body more beautiful when it is more symmetrical. It is tempting to suppose therefore that symmetry could provide an objective basis for beauty.

As it turns out, the supposition that beauty is symmetry is not new. The third-century-BCE Egyptian philosopher Plotinus considered and rejected this theory, for several reasons.

Picture your favorite color. You may call it beautiful even when you conceive of it as a formless patch or color, without any shape, symmetrical or otherwise. Likewise, the precious metal gold is widely considered beautiful, independent of any particular form it may take. What about lightning, the starry sky, and fire? These sights fill our hearts with awe and admiration, though it is hard to think of anything less symmetrical.

Examples like these led Plotinus to suspect that what we recognize as beauty comes from a principle more remote than symmetry. Note that we never see perfect symmetry in the world around us. Every face, every temple, every song approximates this mathematical ideal with greater or less accuracy. Symmetry is defined as exactly equal parts facing each other around an axis. But where does exact equality exist? Only in Plato's world of forms, which we encountered in chapter 1.

Plotinus believed Plato was correct to suppose that the human mind grasps the objects of sensation through abstract ideas. We can understand that *this* lightning bolt and *that* lightning bolt belong in the same category by understanding the abstract idea of lightning, which they have in common. But how do we come to understand that lightning, the starry sky, and fire are all beautiful? It must be that they have the principle of beauty in common. So, although the world of forms provides the abstract ideas that objects of sensation have in common, there must be something beyond the world of forms that provides the final principle that abstract ideas have in common. Plotinus identified this final principle as *Beauty* itself.

For Plotinus, Beauty is the absolute reality beyond the world of forms. It is the single transcendent exemplar of all being. Objects around us are beautiful to the extent that they reflect the absolute reality of Beauty. In other words, the amount of beauty we perceive in an object depends on how well the object can reveal Beauty through itself. We call something "ugly" only to the extent that it provides a poor reflection of that absolute reality. Since Beauty is the highest value in every category, it is identical to the good, the just, and the true. Although Plotinus sometimes called it "god," most often, he called it The One.

Sen no Rikyū—Imperfection

Plotinus's conception of The One is an unchanging, eternal absolute that lends value to the world of forms, which in turn lends stability to the world of change. Beauty itself is what all forms have in common, and the form of lightning is what all lightning bolts have in common. This hierarchy of meaning enables us to speak about and understand the physical world.

Some would insist, however, that the hierarchy is an invention and the understanding it affords is illusory. As we saw in chapter 6, Nagarjuna resisted the urge to posit any stabilizing reality beyond the physical world. He promoted the Buddhist perspective that, since there is no accurate way to capture our constantly changing experiences in language, there is no ultimate truth.

Zen is a form of Buddhism strongly influenced by Daoism, the Chinese nature philosophy we discussed in chapters 5 and 8. Disillusioned with language, Zen Buddhists concentrate on the meaning of life through meditation and a slow, deliberate lifestyle. Crucial to this mindfulness is the appreciation of beauty. The 16th-century Japanese philosopher Sen no Rikyū developed two key aspects of the Zen aesthetic.

The first was the concept of *wabi-sabi*, which means accepting imperfection. Rikyū was an eminent tea master. When he started his career, it was popular to gather in elaborate tea houses and use fancy dishes by the light of the full moon. Rikyū, in contrast, served tea in rustic ceramics in a tiny hut under a waxing, waning, or cloud-streaked moon. He taught that true beauty eliminates all things unnecessary and showy, focusing instead on the transient flow of life.

The related concept of *kintsugi* means embracing the flawed. One day, Rikyū was invited to dinner at the home of a man who wished to show off his expensive jar. Rikyū admired the dying tree outside the window instead. The man was so angry he smashed the jar to pieces. His servants collected the pieces and repaired the jar with golden glue that highlighted the cracks. When Rikyū saw it, he said, *"Now* it is beautiful." The repaired jar celebrated the Zen principles that nothing lasts, nothing is finished, and nothing is perfect.

Rikyū said, "Though many people drink tea, if you do not know the Way of Tea, tea will drink you up." Perhaps he meant that being mindful is the only way to avoid getting carried away by the frenetic concerns of the world. He recommended simplifying to the point of disappearance, where beauty disintegrates to nothing but sublime emptiness.

George Santayana— The Object of Pleasure

Despite their diametrically opposed positions on perfection versus imperfection, Plotinus and Rikyū are united in seeing beauty as objective. For Plotinus, we should begin by contemplating lightning bolts, proceed to contemplating the form of lightning, and end by contemplating the absolute beauty all forms have in common. For Rikyū, we should begin by clearing our minds of showy falsehoods, proceed to clearing our minds of anything unnecessary, and end with the ultimate beauty of absolute nothingness. Moving in opposite directions, both Plotinus and Rikyū proposed universal definitions of beauty.

The 19th-century Spanish-American philosopher George Santayana, in contrast, presented a subjective account. In his view, sometimes called *aesthetic hedonism*, beauty is a source of pleasure. Since different things please different people, we should not expect a universal definition of beauty. To say that the experience of beauty is subjective, however, is not to deny its special status. According to Santayana, human beings have a "sense of beauty" that is different from our experience of other pleasures.

For example, suppose you go to a performance of Beethoven's Symphony No. 9 and have a pleasurable experience. You listen to a pop song on the radio in the car on the way home and find it pleasurable as well. Yet you might be more likely to call the symphony beautiful but not the pop song. Why?

According to Santayana, the symphony gives you the kind of pleasure you feel everyone ought to appreciate. With the pop song, on the other hand, you recognize that different people have different tastes. Likewise for a beautiful painting at a museum versus a mass-produced painting on the wall of a hotel room. We feel someone who values hotel paintings over museum paintings, or pop songs over symphonies, is missing something important.

As Santayana cautioned, however, the feeling that "everyone ought to appreciate it" is itself subjective. Although the feeling may be real, it is based on the culture, education, and general psychology of the individual. To judge something beautiful is to affirm an ideal—a preference we expect everyone to share.

Santayana asserted that a melody is more beautiful than the pure tone of a tuning fork. In other words, he expects people to find more pleasure in the melody than in the pure tone. But we are often wrong about our expectations, which accounts for the many spirited debates we have about beauty. (After all, Rikyū might actually prefer the pure tone of a tuning fork!) In the end, Santayana would say that everything is potentially beautiful because everything is capable of producing that special pleasure for someone.

Iris Murdoch—The Object of Love

The 20th-century Irish-British philosopher Iris Murdoch agreed with Santayana that we have a special sense of beauty. In her view, however, beauty has a much more important job than simply giving pleasure. Beauty is the name for things in art and nature that have the power to change our consciousness.

Picture yourself in a terrible mood, staring blankly out the window. Then something catches your eye. It is a kestrel, with its wings arched and tail splayed, hanging magically in the air. You gasp. In an instant, everything is changed. The brooding self has disappeared. There is nothing now but the kestrel. And then, after the kestrel swoops down for its prey and flies off, whatever was bothering you seems less important. You feel released from your petty little life.

Murdoch called this kind of experience *unselfing*. Recall from chapter 10 how Ayn Rand argued that all rational human behavior is selfish. Murdoch would grant that we are prone to obsessing over our own lives, but she would find fault with Rand for regarding this obsession as a virtue. Becoming virtuous requires the ability to look upon humanity with unselfish love.

Though we find beauty in both nature and in art, according to Murdoch, the beauty in art is especially conducive to virtue. Picture yourself at a gallery gazing at a beautiful painting of a hovering kestrel. Just like the real kestrel, the painted kestrel unselfs you, but at the same time it also unites you with others—the painter and all those who appreciate the painting. Encountering beauty in nature *can* be social in this way, but it is more likely to be solitary—a fleeting glimpse that is difficult to share.

CHAPTER THIRTEEN

What Is Art?

When we teach children to draw, we typically assume that art is *mimesis*—imitation of the real world. If the child fails to draw a nose at the center of a face, we may encourage the child to correct the drawing. However, mimesis is only one very narrow conception of what art is. In the 18th century, people may have especially admired painters who could paint a face with photographic accuracy or musicians who could play an instrument to sound like a bird. Given that modern technology enables us to copy the real world with absolute precision, it is not surprising to find us looking for much more than mimesis in art.

But what exactly are we looking for?

Georg Hegel—Ideal Beauty

When we think of great art, often the first thing that comes to mind are the sumptuous oil paintings we see hanging in museums. Take, for example, *Aristotle with a Bust of Homer* by Rembrandt van Rijn. It depicts the ancient Greek philosopher Aristotle, whom we discussed in chapter 1, reaching out to a statue of Homer, author of the *Iliad* and the *Odyssey*, the first great literary works of Western civilization.

Even if we did not grasp the epic importance of the two men depicted, the painting would dazzle us. The luster of Aristotle's jewelry, the shimmer of his cape, the graceful strength of his posture, the wisdom on his face—these features and more make the painting beautiful. Rembrandt's Aristotle is not very realistic (for example, his costume is historically incorrect); on the contrary, he portrays an ideal.

The idealist philosophy of Georg Hegel in the 19th century provided an interesting explanation of our appreciation of art like Rembrandt's. Recall from chapter 1 that idealists view ideas as more real than the physical world. Whereas Plato thought ideas are eternal forms in another realm, Hegel argued that they are the rational principles organizing matter. Because reason is the common denominator among ideas, reason is the ultimate reality and it is most perfectly realized in humanity. Reason has come to life in us. Hegel therefore considered reason to be a kind of world spirit. Human history is the story of this world spirit slowly emerging and working its way toward absolute freedom.

Looking at the history of art, Hegel noted how primitive art represented humans as stiff and static. It was ancient Greek art that first began to show what dynamic self-determination we are capable of. Since then, art has increasingly depicted the movement and power of the human body, making our freedom of spirit ever more evident. The genius of Old Masters such as Rembrandt or Vermeer was to depict this freedom without sacrificing the calm dignity that reason affords.

For Hegel, an active pose of the human form, such as Rembrandt's Aristotle, best reminds us of our inner freedom. Other compositions, such as a galloping horse or even a bountiful tray of fruit, could also provide an experience of reason in dynamic self-determination. Likewise, other arts, such as music and drama, can reveal our own true nature as part of the world spirit. Art strikes us as beautiful because we see our ideal selves in it. Any production that cannot remind us of our ideal selves should not be counted as art in Hegel's view.

Leo Tolstoy--Shared Emotion

Hegel rejected mimesis. According to him, art should not present the real but the ideal. The 19th-century Russian philosopher Leo Tolstoy, in contrast, was a master of realistic fiction. Yet, in writing lifelike drama, his goal was not just to reflect humanity, but to unite us. He was nominated for the Nobel Prize for literature and the Nobel Peace Prize several times.

Tolstoy believed art enables one person to communicate his or her feelings to another in a way that eliminates the distinction between the two minds, creating a single consciousness between them. Artists "infect" others with what they feel. The strength of the infection, and hence the greatness of the art, depends on three conditions: individuality, clearness, and sincerity.

Tolstoy's three conditions for great art are amply illustrated in one of his own famous novels, *Anna Karenina*. Its central character is a woman named Anna, who has a forbidden love affair and suffers so much for it that she feels compelled to throw herself under a train. Tolstoy wrote this novel after learning that the rejected mistress of one of his married friends had thrown herself under a train. Tolstoy saw the woman's crushed body with his own eyes at the train station. The experience shook him to the core; he wanted to understand her. In the novel, he got inside Anna's head, trying to show how her weaknesses led to her demise. He also inserted himself into the story through the contrasting character, Levin, who painstakingly transformed his weaknesses into strength.

Anna Karenina is a long read, with many stretches that are neither pretty nor pleasant. Nevertheless, if Tolstoy was right, the emotional investment is worthwhile. When you are the viewer of a great painting or the reader of a great book, you should be so authentically moved that you feel you could have produced the work yourself. Art expresses what you have all along been needing to express, without even being aware of this need.

Tolstoy viewed sincerity as the most important of his three conditions for artistic infection. He despised upper-class art, like the Old Masters paintings admired by Hegel, on the grounds that it is produced to stroke the vanity of the wealthy and powerful. In fact, the Russian Orthodox Church excommunicated Tolstoy for repudiating the pomp and circumstance in religion and for interpreting Jesus's message in a subversively simplified way. For Tolstoy, the shared emotion art evinces must be morally pure. In his view, morality was best understood through the

Christian gospels, but he allowed that there could be other sincerely spiritual perspectives.

Friedrich Nietzsche–Inventing Value

Despite his success as a novelist, Tolstoy did not feel his work met his own aesthetic standards. Although he tried to share his morality through his characters, they had a way of taking on a life of their own, defying his ability to control their message. For example, he wanted to condemn Anna Karenina's impulsive love, yet he wrote her with such vibrant sympathy that she has become one of the most celebrated fictional characters in history. Although this was a sign of failure to Tolstoy, Friedrich Nietzsche would approve.

Nietzsche saw a model for artistic achievement in ancient Greek tragedy. All across ancient Greece, people gathered in outdoor theaters to watch tragic plays that retold myths about the gods. Unlike modern plays, ancient Greek plays had a very formal structure, alternating between spoken dialogue and musical chorus. Nietzsche argued that this contrast taught the perfect balance for a healthy outlook on life. The dialogue represented logic, which was associated with Apollo, the god of order and reason. Meanwhile, the chorus represented passion, which was associated with Dionysus, the god of chaos and ecstasy. Since they worshiped these gods, the ancient Greeks took the symbolic message of their tragic plays very seriously: we need both order and chaos to be fully human.

According to Nietzsche, the goal of Socrates, whom we met in the introduction to this book, was to glorify order while banishing chaos. Socrates's emphasis on the importance of reason sent Western culture on a quest for understanding that ignores our need to dance and sing and run wild. This obsession with reason came to a climax in Hegel, who christened reason as the world spirit and worshiped it as the divine within us. Critical of such extreme rationalism, Nietzsche felt that great art, such as the dramatic operas of Richard Wagner or the romantic novels of Tolstoy, should help bring our creatively irrational impulses back into the picture.

As we reject traditional morality, we must invent new value. This is the true purpose of art, in Nietzsche's view, making art the highest form of human activity. Nietzsche was scathingly critical of the common Christian values Tolstoy wished to promote. Nietzsche saw Christianity as a slave religion, which made people subservient and kept them from realizing their full potential. Knowing it was too late to return to the ancient Greek religion, Nietzsche famously announced that "God is dead" in an effort to make way for a new cultural ideal.

Nietzsche wanted us to see our lives as great works of art. As artists, we should strive to transcend nature. Consider the fact that human beings have evolved from apelike ancestors—and we are not yet finished evolving. Looking forward into the future, we must ask—what are we capable of becoming? Only artistic genius can imagine the possibilities. In his own philosophical novel, Nietzsche proposed the ideal of the *Übermensch*, or "overman," an independent, fearless lover of life, who feels no shame but rather enjoys and celebrates his own abilities.

Virginia Woolf—An Infinite Difficulty for Women

In this chapter, we have been examining authors from the 19th century, when the concept of artistic genius emerged. Although some argued that genius is an inborn gift (Hegel) and others argued that it is the product of diligent effort (Nietzsche), everyone seemed to agree with Tolstoy that a genius is a "force producing effects beyond the scope of ordinary human agencies." The 19th-century philosopher Arthur Schopenhauer memorably remarked that "talent hits a target no one else can hit; genius hits a target no one else can see."

It was not until the 20th century that women began to express concern about the male monopoly on genius. Plato showed no bias against the female mind, inviting women to study philosophy at his Academy and picturing women and men alike as philosopher-kings in his ideal society. But Plato's progressive attitude did not take root. It was over-shadowed by Aristotle's biological account of the female as an underdeveloped male, which supported a long legacy of sexism in philosophy, science, and art.

The area of the art world where women first made their biggest impact was in novel writing (for example, Jane Austen, the Brontë sisters, and Louisa May Alcott), but even here, progress has been slow. The 20th-century English novelist Virginia Woolf put her finger on the problem when she gave a famous speech about Judith Shakespeare, the imaginary sister of William Shakespeare.

Judith, we might imagine, is just as talented as her brother. Yet she is not so fortunate as he. After running away in order to escape her family's pressure to marry, she is impregnated by a man who claimed he would help her career. Frustration at every turn eventually drives Judith to suicide.

Although Woolf imagined this tragedy occurring during the Renaissance, in her extended essay, *A Room of One's Own*, she cautioned her listeners that the same story could be told in their own day, the 1920s: "Now my belief is that this poet who never wrote a word and was buried at the cross-roads still lives. She lives in you and in me, and in many other women who are not here to-night, for they are washing up the dishes and putting the children to bed."

Woolf prods us to ask ourselves: does Judith still live with us today—100 years later, in the 2020s?

Woolf, whose sister was a painter, saw painting and writing as two sides of the same coin. Speaking from personal experience, she asserted that it is infinitely difficult for a woman in our male-dominated society to discover her genius and produce great art.

John Dewey—A Meaningful Experience

But perhaps the problem lies in accepting the concept of the artistic genius in the first place. The 20th-century American philosopher John Dewey strove to bring art out of the museums and concert halls and into our homes and backyards. For him, art should not be thought of as a rare and expensive national treasure but as a regular part of ordinary life.

Dewey believed every one of us should devote some time and energy to producing art. It doesn't have to be "great." Art is a way of focusing on an experience to make it more meaningful. In particular, the artist's job is to take a passionate reaction to some aspect of life and refine it into harmonious order. This work is a very satisfying process, and crucial for human happiness.

Dewey illustrated his conception of art through the example of the poem "Tintern Abbey" by William Wordsworth. Tintern Abbey is a beautiful ruin of a monastery in the English countryside. Wordsworth had visited it five years prior as a carefree young man. Upon his return, he had matured, and enjoyed the same ruin in a deeper way. He wrote:

> For I have learned
> To look on nature, not as in the hour
> Of thoughtless youth; but hearing oftentimes
> The still sad music of humanity

In Dewey's view, the circumstances in which Wordsworth wrote "Tintern Abbey" are of the utmost importance. Writing the poem helped Wordsworth make sense of his reaction to his second visit to the monastery. It created a harmonious resolution for him. But this harmonious resolution, being a thing of beauty itself, became something to share with others. As readers, our enjoyment of the poem becomes a new experience for us, which we may return to years later, just as Wordsworth returned to Tintern Abbey.

So, for Dewey, art is not an object. The object we call "art" is really just a touchstone for a series of interconnected experiences. A child's noseless drawing might create a more meaningful experience for you than the work of an Old Master. Art is the meaningful experience that you and the artist create together through some object of beauty.

What can make artwork like an Old Master's especially meaningful, however, is the way its exceptional beauty can connect so many different people across the ages. Think of how many people have enjoyed *Aristotle with a Bust of Homer*, "Tintern Abbey," or *Anna Karenina*. Though our experiences of such a work are diverse, they are united by the work itself, which forms a valuable bond among us.

Dewey warned, however, that the special meaning of art emerges only when we are genuinely moved by its beauty. If we ogle a work simply because it is famous or expensive, art does not happen. Dewey urged us to make art happen, both by finding artistic ways to express our passionate reactions and by enjoying the artistic expressions of others.

THOUGHT EXPERIMENT
THE FOUR RED SQUARES

From the 20th-century American philosopher Arthur Danto. Imagine an abstract painting by an artist such as Piet Mondrian at the Museum of Modern Art in New York City. It is nothing but a single red square. Yet it is worth a lot of money and is internationally celebrated as a great work of art.

Surely, you are capable of painting a red square indistinguishable from the Mondrian. Would your red square count as art? The Museum of Modern Art is not likely to add it to their collection. What makes it different from the Mondrian? Does it need meaning?

Imagine a third red square, indistinguishable from the first two. It is a standard storm advisory issued by the weather service. Although it has a meaning, it is not art. What makes it different from the Mondrian? Does it need artistic intention?

Imagine a fourth red square. It is a painting by a young aspiring artist called *Kierkegaard's Anguish*, on display at a minor gallery. Although it has an artistic intention, it is not internationally celebrated as a great work of art. Why not?

How do we judge artistic value?

Closing Thoughts

In this book, we have journeyed far and wide across the colorful landscape of philosophy. We've gone back in time to some of the earliest recorded philosophical ideas. We've also traveled around the globe. Looking back on all the thinkers we have explored, it is hard not to be impressed by the diversity of opinions about reality, knowledge, and values. It is also reassuring to see that, in all their diverse opinions, these philosophers were essentially doing the same thing—searching for answers to the deepest questions about life.

Every one of us has an interest in seeking wisdom. We all need to do it and we want to do it, once we discover how rewarding it is.

The disadvantage of such a wide-ranging book as this is that it can only skim the surface of so many intriguing theories. But it is meant to be a starting point. On the following pages, you will find resources that can take you deeper into the philosophers who especially interest you.

Just think how pleased these thinkers would have been to know that a future person, like *you*, cares about what they thought. In the same way, there may be other people, present and future, who care about what *you* think. In caring about the perspectives of others, we demonstrate that humanity is trying to improve. And that matters—regardless of how much we discover or how long we last.

Do you think philosophy can help us become a noble species? Would this be a worthy goal? What would your conception of a noble species look like? What would you need to do to help make it happen?

Resources

1000-Word Philosophy: An Introductory Anthology. 1000WordPhilosophy.com

Encyclopedia Britannica. Britannica.com

Internet Encyclopedia of Philosophy. IEP.utm.edu

New World Encyclopedia. NewWorldEncyclopedia.org

Russell, Bertrand. *The History of Western Philosophy.* New York: Simon and Schuster, 1945. Archive.org /details/TheHistoryOfWesternPhilosophy

Stanford Encyclopedia of Philosophy. Plato.Stanford .edu/index.html

References

Audi, Robert. *Epistemology: A Contemporary Introduction to the Theory of Knowledge,* 3rd ed. New York: Routledge, 2010.

Bernstein, Lenny. "We Eat 100 Acres of Pizza a Day in the U.S." *The Washington Post,* January 20, 2015. WashingtonPost.com/news/to-your-health/wp/2015/01/20/we-eat-100-acres-of-pizza-a-day-in-the-u-s.

Cahn, Steven M., and Peter J. Markie. *Ethics: History, Theory, and Contemporary Issues*, 6th Ed. New York: Oxford University Press, 2015.

Copi, Irving M. *Introduction to Logic*, 14th ed. New York: Pearson, 2014.

Kim, Jaegwon, Daniel Z. Korman, and Ernest Sosa, eds. *Metaphysics: An Anthology.* 2nd ed. Malden, MA: Wiley-Blackwell, 2012.

Leaman, Oliver. *Eastern Philosophy: Key Readings.* New York: Routledge, 2000.

Shafer-Landau, Russ, ed. *Ethical Theory: An Anthology.* 2nd ed. Malden, MA: Wiley-Blackwell, 2013.

Sosa, Ernest, Jaegwon Kim, Jeremy Fantl, and Matthew McGrath, eds. *Epistemology: An Anthology.* 2nd ed. Malden, MA: Wiley-Blackwell, 2008.

van Inwagen, Peter, and Dean W. Zimmerman, eds. *Metaphysics: The Big Questions.* 2nd ed. Malden, MA: Wiley-Blackwell, 2008.

Index

Acknowledgment

I would like to thank John Carroll University for supporting my work on this project.

About the Author

 **Sharon Kaye** is a professor in the Department of Philosophy at John Carroll University in Cleveland, Ohio. She graduated Phi Beta Kappa from the University of Wisconsin, Madison, in 1992. After receiving her PhD in 1997 from the University of Toronto, she was a Killam postdoctoral fellow at Dalhousie University in Halifax, Nova Scotia. Since then, she has published numerous articles as well as books, including *Big Thinkers and Big Ideas: An Introduction to Eastern and Western Philosophy for Kids* (2020), *Philosophy for Teens* volumes I and II with Paul Thomson (2006, 2007), *Critical Thinking: A Beginner's Guide* (2009), and *Philosophy: A Complete Introduction* (2014). Her works have been translated into Japanese, Greek, Turkish, Spanish, Portuguese, and Slovak. She is currently writing the K-12 philosophy curriculum for Royal Fireworks Press. She directs a Philosophy for Kids program that enables undergraduates to lead philosophy discussions for gifted middle school students. She is raising two children, two dogs, a cat, and a gecko.